First World War
and Army of Occupation
War Diary
France, Belgium and Germany

60 DIVISION
Divisional Troops
1/6 London Field Company Royal Engineers
1 December 1915 - 30 November 1916

WO95/3028/1

The Naval & Military Press Ltd
www.nmarchive.com
Published in association with The National Archives

Published by

The Naval & Military Press Ltd

Unit 10 Ridgewood Industrial Park,

Uckfield, East Sussex,

TN22 5QE England

Tel: +44 (0) 1825 749494

www.naval-military-press.com

www.nmarchive.com

This diary has been reprinted in facsimile from the original. Any imperfections are inevitably reproduced and the quality may fall short of modern type and cartographic standards.

© Crown Copyright
Images reproduced by permission of The National Archives, London, England, 2015.

Contents

Document type	Place/Title	Date From	Date To
Heading	WO95/3028/1		
Heading	60th Division 1-6th London Fld Coy RE 1915 Dec-1916 Nov		
Heading	War Diary Of 1/6th London Field Company Royal Engineers From 1st December 1915 To 31st December 1915		
War Diary	Bishop's Stortford	01/12/1915	31/12/1915
Heading	War Diary Of 1/6 London Field Company, Royal Engineers, 60th (London) Division, From 1st March, 1916 To 31st March, 1916 Volume VI		
War Diary	Sutton Veny	01/03/1916	31/03/1916
Heading	War Diary Of 1/6th London Field Company Royal Engineers (T) 60th (London) Division From 1st April 1916 To 30th April 1916 Volume V		
War Diary	Sutton Veny	01/04/1916	30/04/1916
Miscellaneous	Appendix A	08/04/1916	08/04/1916
Miscellaneous	Appendix B 1/6th London Field CO.R.E.	15/04/1916	15/04/1916
Miscellaneous	Appendix C Promotions.		
Miscellaneous	Appendix D 1/6th London Field CO.R.E.	22/04/1916	22/04/1916
Miscellaneous	Appendix E 1/6th London Field Company. R.E.	29/04/1916	29/04/1916
Heading	War Diary Of 1/6th London Field Company, Royal Engineers, 60th (London) Division From 1st May, 1916 To 31st May 1916 Volume VI		
War Diary	Sutton Veny	01/05/1916	29/05/1916
Miscellaneous	Appendix A 1/6th London Field Company.R.E.	06/05/1916	06/05/1916
War Diary	Sutton Veny	30/05/1916	31/05/1916
Miscellaneous	Appendix B 1/6th London Field Company.R.E.	13/05/1916	13/05/1916
Miscellaneous	Appendix C 1/6th London Field Company.R.E.	20/05/1916	20/05/1916
Miscellaneous	Appendix D 1/6th. London Field Company.R.E.	27/05/1916	27/05/1916
Miscellaneous	Appendix E 1/6th. London Field Company.R.E.	29/05/1916	29/05/1916
Miscellaneous	Appendix F Transfers.	11/05/1915	11/05/1915
Miscellaneous	Appendix G	16/05/1916	16/05/1916
Miscellaneous	Appendix H Transfers.	22/05/1916	22/05/1916
Miscellaneous	Appendix I Transfers.	23/05/1916	23/05/1916
Heading	War Diary Of 1/6th London Field Company Royal Engineers 60th (London) Division From 1st June 1916 To 22nd June 1916 Volume VII		
War Diary	Sutton Veny	01/06/1916	22/06/1916
Miscellaneous	Appendix A 1/6th London. Field Company.R.E.	29/05/1916	29/05/1916
Miscellaneous	Appendix B 1/6th London Field Company.R.E.	05/06/1916	05/06/1916
Miscellaneous	Appendix C 1/6th London Field Company.R.E.	12/06/1916	12/06/1916
War Diary	Sutton Veny	23/06/1916	23/06/1916
War Diary	Southampton	23/06/1916	23/06/1916
War Diary	Havre	24/06/1916	25/06/1916
War Diary	St Pol	26/06/1916	26/06/1916
War Diary	Haute-Cote	27/06/1916	27/06/1916
War Diary	Fm Doffine	28/06/1916	28/06/1916
War Diary	Mont St Eloy	29/06/1916	30/06/1916
Miscellaneous	Cavalry Artillery And Infantry Only	30/06/1916	30/06/1916
Miscellaneous	Officers Absent On duty	29/06/1916	29/06/1916

War Diary	Mont St Eloy	30/06/1916	08/07/1916
War Diary	Ferme Doffine	10/07/1916	10/07/1916
War Diary	Mont St Eloy	10/07/1916	30/07/1916
Heading	1/6th London Field Coy RE War Diary August 1916		
War Diary	Mont St Eloy	01/08/1916	31/08/1916
Miscellaneous	Appendix I 1/6th London Field Co.R.E.	26/08/1916	26/08/1916
Heading	War Diary Of 1/6th London Field Coy R.E. (T.F.) September 1916		
War Diary	Mont St Eloy	01/09/1916	30/09/1916
Miscellaneous	Appendix		
Heading	War Diary Of 1/6th London Field Co. RE (T) 1st To 31st October 1916		
War Diary	Mont St Eloy	01/10/1916	24/10/1916
War Diary	Penin	24/10/1916	26/10/1916
War Diary	Moncheaux	27/10/1916	28/10/1916
War Diary	Bonnieres	29/10/1916	29/10/1916
War Diary	Famechon	30/10/1916	31/10/1916
Miscellaneous	Appendices		
Miscellaneous	Appendix 5		
Miscellaneous	Appendix 3		
Heading	War Diary Of 1/6th London Field Coy R.E. 1st To 30th November 1916 Vol 6		
War Diary	Famechon	01/11/1916	02/11/1916
War Diary	Lemeillard	03/11/1916	03/11/1916
War Diary	Bussus Bussue	04/11/1916	21/11/1916
War Diary	Marseilles	21/11/1916	30/11/1916

WO 95/3028/

60TH DIVISION

1-6TH LONDON FLD COY R.E.

1915 DEC — 1916 NOV

To SALONIKA
RE NUMBERED 519 (1917 FEB)

CONFIDENTIAL.

WAR DIARY OF

1/6TH LONDON FIELD COMPANY, ROYAL ENGINEERS.

from 1st December 1915 to 31st December 1915.

Volume I.

Army Form C.2118.

WAR DIARY
OF
1/6TH LONDON FIELD COMPANY, ROYAL ENGINEERS

HOUR, DATE, PLACE.		SUMMARY OF EVENTS AND INFORMATION.	REMARKS AND REFERENCE TO APPENDICES.
1.12.15.	Bishop's Stortford.	Technical Training. ALSA MEADOW. Horses 17551 and 17572 transferred from 2/4th Fld. Coy.	JRC
2.12.15.	ditto.	Horses cast by A.D.V.S., 17453 and 17439. Technical Training RIVER STORT 2nd Lieut.W.H.Lee to attend Farriery Course at Bishop's Stortford instead of 2nd Lieut.G.W.Bacon.	Authority H.Q., G349 dated 30.11.15 JRC
3.12.15.	ditto.	Technical Training. ALSA MEADOW. Spr.Rumbold discharged medically unfit for Service.	Authority W.O.Letter No. DAGE, B/5663 - 1.12.15. JRC
4.12.15.	ditto.	Company Drill. SILVERLEYS.	JRC
5.12.15	DITTO.	Church Parade. ST MICHAEL'S CHURCH.	JRC
6.12.15.	ditto.	Technical Training ALSA MEADOW. Lecture in Bombing SILVERLEYS. Capt. F.R.Cullingford returned from Sick Leave this day.	JRC
7.12.15.	ditto.	Technical Training BASSINGBOURNE HALL Order re Bombing read first time.	JRC

Army Form C.2118.

WAR DIARY

OF

1/6TH LONDON FIELD COMPANY, ROYAL ENGINEERS

HOUR, DATE, PLACE.		SUMMARY OF EVENTS AND INFORMATION.	REMARKS AND REFERENCE TO APPENDICES.
8.12.15.	Bishop's Stortford.	Technical Training RIVER STORT. Order re Bounds read 2nd time.	JRC
9.12.15.	ditto.	Technical Training SILVERLEYS. Transfer of S.&.C.S.Simpson from 3/4th Fld.Coy. Promotion of S.&.C.S.Simpson to Far.Sgt. Order re Bounds read 3rd time.	Authority T.F.Records No.A.M.R 615, dated 2.12.15. JRC
10.12.15.	ditto.	Technical Training ALSA MEADOW. Order re Postal Arrangements read 1st time. Pnr.Spicer remusted as Sapper. Transfer of Pte.W.S.Bucknell from 18th Batt.Lon.Regt.	JRC Authority T.F.Records 3342/JRC R.E.9/6.12.15 JRC
11.12.15.	ditto.	Company Drill SILVERLEYS.	JRC
12.12.15.	ditto.	Church Parade. ST MICHAEL'S CHURCH.	JRC
13.12.15.	ditto.	Technical Training. ALSA MEADOW. Lecture:- Care of Arms C.4.M.STORES.	JRC

Army Form C.2118.

WAR DIARY
of
1/6TH LONDON FIELD COMPANY, ROYAL ENGINEERS

HOUR, DATE, PLACE.		SUMMARY OF EVENTS AND INFORMATION.	REMARKS AND REFERENCES TO APPENDICES.
14.12.15.	Bishop's Stortford.	Technical Training C.Q.M.STORES. Lecture:- March Discipline DAME-O-GOYS FARM.	JRC
15.12.15.	ditto.	Route March :- LITTLE HADHAM, CLAPGATE, UPWICK GREEN, LEVELS GREEN. Transfer of Cpl.Holloway from 2/4th Fld.Coy. Promotion of Cpl. Holloway to Sgt.(Acting)	Authority T.F.Records 5269/R.E.2 14.12.15 JRC
16.12.15.	ditto.	Technical Training RIVER STORT Pnr.Nichols and Pnr.Streeter return from Cookery Course.	JRC
17.12.15.	ditto.	Technical Training. RIVER STORT & AISA MEADOW. Spr.Bevis transferred to R.E.H.S.Details Colchester	Authority T.F.Records No.5433 R.E.2 dated 8.12.15. JRC
18.12.15.	ditto.	Company & Saluting Drill, SILVERLEYS.	JRC
19.12.15.	ditto.	Church Parade, ST. MICHAELS CHURCH.	JRC

Army Form C.2118.

WAR DIARY

OF

1/6TH LONDON FIELD COMPANY, ROYAL ENGINEERS.

HOUR, DATE, PLACE.		SUMMARY OF EVENTS AND INFORMATION.	REMARKS AND REFERENCE TO APPENDICES.
20.12.15.	Bishop's Stortford.	Technical Training ALSA MEADOW. Musketry. SILVERLEY'S RIFLE RANGE & C.Q.M.STORES.	JRC
21.12.15.	ditto.	Technical Training SILVERLEY'S RIFLE RANGE. Lecture DANE-O-COYS FARM. Order re Dress read out first time.	JRC
22.12.15.	ditto.	Technical Training ALBA MEADOW. Pnr.Wright discharged under para.392 ii Kings Regulations. Promotion of Lce.Cpl.Allingham to Act.Cpl. " " Driver Hooker to Lce.Cpl. " " " Hayden to " " Order re Dress read out second time. 2nd Lieut.G.W.Bacon granted 7 days Sick Leave.	Authority a.F.Records letter 20.12.15. W.O.Letter 0/255 (A.G.2.B.) dated 6.12.15. JRC
23.12.15.	ditto.	Technical Training RIVER SPORT. Lecture DANE-O-COYS FARM. Order re Dress read out third time.	JRC
24.12.15.	ditto.	Inspection by MAJOR GENERAL BULFIN C.V.O., C.B. Technical Training ALSA MEADOW. Received instructions per telephone re move to Brightlingsea for training in Pontoon and other Bridging.	JRC
25.12.15.	ditto.	Check Parade C.Q.M.STORES. Instructions re move confirmed.	JRC

Army Form C.2118

WAR DIARY

OF

1/6TH LONDON FIELD COMPANY, ROYAL ENGINEERS.

HOUR, DATE, PLACE.		SUMMARY OF EVENTS AND INFORMATION.	REMARKS AND REFERENCE TO APPENDICES.
26.12.15.	Bishop's Stortford.	Church Parade ST MICHAEL'S CHURCH.	JRC
27.12.15.	ditto.	Check Parade, C.Q.M.STORES.	JRC
28.12.15.	ditto.	Technical Training, SILVERLEYS AND ALSA MEADOW. 2nd Lieuts W.H.Lee and E.H.Targett and Cpl. Kirkpatrick to attend Course in Musketry. 2nd Lieut. G.W.Bacon granted Sick Leave.(7 days)	JRC
29.12.15.	ditto.	Technical Training, SILVERLEYS Lecture, DANE-O-COYS FARM.	JRC
30.12.15.	ditto.	Technical Training, ALSA MEADOW & DANE-O-COYS FARM 2nd Lieut. E.H.J.Stewart to attend Farriery Course. Received Pontoon and Trestle Waggons.	Authority Headqrs.Div.letter G349/13 dated 22.12.15. JRC
31.12.15.	ditto.	Technical Training C.Q.M.STORES & ALSA MEADOW Sprs. Bone & Carter to attend Farriery Course.	Authority Headqrs.Letter G313/24 dated 30.12.15. JRC

C O N F I D E N T I A L.

W A R   D I A R Y   O F

1/6th LONDON FIELD COMPANY, ROYAL ENGINEERS, 60th (LONDON) DIVISION.

FROM 1st MARCH, 1916 to 31st MARCH, 1916

----------oOo----------

VOLUME IV.

Army Form C. 2118.

WAR DIARY

~~INTELLIGENCE SUMMARY~~

(Erase heading not required.)

Instructions regarding War Diaries and Intelligence Summaries are contained in F. S. Regs., Part II. and the Staff Manual respectively. Title pages will be prepared in manuscript.

Place	Date	Hour	Summary of Events and Information	Remarks and references to Appendices
SUTTON VENY	1916 1.3	9-4	Earthworks and instructing Working Parties from 180th Infantry Brigade at SUTTON VENY Trenches.	
do	2.3	"	do.	
do	3.3	"	do.	
do	4.3	9-12	Road Repairs in Camp.	
do	5.3	10.45 a.m.	Church Parade.	
			2nd.Lieut. G.W.BACON returned from Course of Mounted Duties at ALDERSHOT.	
			2nd.Lieut. C.F.BUDENBERG proceeded to do. do.	
do	6.3	9-4	Earthworks and Instructing, &c.	
			2nd.Lieut.W.B.BACON granted Leave from 6.3.16. to 10.3.16.	
do	7.3	9-4	Earthworks, etc.	
do	8.3	9-4	Earthworks, etc. and Musketry Instruction.	
			13 Sappers and one driver transferred from 3/2nd London Divisional Engineers (Nominal Roll Appendix A, para: 1.)	See "A"
do	9.3	9-4	Earthworks, etc. and Musketry Instruction.	
do	10.3	9-4	Earthworks, etc. and Musketry Instruction.	
do	11.3	9-4	Musketry Instruction.	
do	12.3	10.45 a.m.	Church Parade	

Army Form C. 2118.

WAR DIARY

or

~~INTELLIGENCE SUMMARY.~~

(Erase heading not required.)

Instructions regarding War Diaries and Intelligence
Summaries are contained in F. S. Regs., Part II.
and the Staff Manual respectively. Title pages
will be prepared in manuscript.

Place	Date	Hour	Summary of Events and Information	Remarks and references to Appendices
SUTTON VENY.	1916			
	13.3	7.30 to 5	General Musketry Course Commenced.	
	14.3	"	General Musketry Course continued.	
			Capt.F.R.CULLINGFORD granted Sick Leave from 8.3.16 to 28.3.16	
			2nd.Lieut.E.H.J.STEWART returned to duty from Sick Leave.	
			4 Sappers transferred from 3/2nd LONDON DIVISIONAL ENGINEERS(Appendix A. para:2).	See "A"
	15.3	"	General Musketry Course continued.	
			4 Sappers transferred to 7th PROVISIONAL FIELD COMPANY.R.E. (Appendix B).	See "B"
	16.3	"	General Musketry Course continued.	
	17.3	8.a.m.	Emergency Alarm practiced in accordance with 60th(London) Divisional Order No.180 dated 9.3.16.	
		7.30 to 5. 0.	General Musketry Course continued.	
	18.3	7.30 to 12.	General Musketry Course continued.	
			(Extract from Third Supplement London Gazette dated 10.3.16):- Capt.F.R.CULLINGFORD relinquishes his position on account of ill health dated 14.3.16.	
	19.3	10.45 a.m.	Church Parade.	
			2nd.Lieut.B.F.NELL proceeded to NEWARK for Course in Field Works.	
	20.3	7.30 to 8	Physical Training.	
		9-4	Earthworks & Instructing Infantry.	

Army Form C. 2118.

WAR DIARY

~~INTELLIGENCE SUMMARY~~

(Erase heading not required.)

Instructions regarding War Diaries and Intelligence Summaries are contained in F.S. Regs., Part II. and the Staff Manual respectively. Title pages will be prepared in manuscript.

Place	Date	Hour	Summary of Events and Information	Remarks and references to Appendices
SUTTON VENY.	1916			
	21.3	7.30 to 8.0	Physical Drill.	
		9-4	Repacking Tool Carts and sorting Technical Stores.	
	22.3	7.30. to 8.	Physical Training.	
		9-4	Repairs of Roads and Stables in R.E.CAMP.	
		1.45.	Emergency Alarm practiced in accordance with 60th(London) Division Order No.180 dated 9.3.16.	
	23.3	7.30. to 8.	Physical Training.	
		9-4	Repairs to Stables in R.E.CAMP.	
	24.3.	7.30. to 8.	Physical Training.	
		9-4.	Earthworks and Instructing Infantry.	
			No.2736.Pnr.LAWFORD proceeded to ROMSEY for Course in Farriery.	
			No.2848.Spr.PASSINGHAM.C.A. discharged medically unfit for Military Service under Para:392 (d.d.)(iii) K.R.	
	25.3	7.30. to.8	Physical Training.	
		9-12	Repairs to Stables in R.E.CAMP.	
			2nd.Lieut.C.F.BUDENBERG returned from Course in Mounted Duties.	
	26.3.	10.45 a.m.	Church Parade.	
			2nd.Lieut.A.H.LEE proceeded to ALDERSHOT for Course in Mounted Duties.	
	27.3	7.30. to 8.	Physical Training.	

Army Form C. 2118.

WAR DIARY

~~INTELLIGENCE~~ SUMMARY

(Erase heading not required.)

Instructions regarding War Diaries and Intelligence
Summaries are contained in F. S. Regs., Part II.
and the Staff Manual respectively. Title pages
will be prepared in manuscript.

Place	Date	Hour	Summary of Events and Information	Remarks and references to Appendices
SUTTON VENY.	1916 27.3.	9-4	Earthworks and Instructing Infantry.	
	28.3.		2nd.Lieut.W.H.LEE granted Leave 27.3.16 to 31.3.16. Outdoor Training cancelled owing to bad weather. Lectures and Musketry Instruction.	
	29.3	7.30. to 8.0. 9-4	Physical Training. Earthworks and Instructing Infantry.	
	30.3.	7.30 to 8. 9-4 6.0. p.m.	Physical Training. Earthworks and Instructing Infantry. March Out with Transport.	
	31.3	7.30 to 8 9-4	Physical Training. Earthworks and Superintending Infantry. No.2.C.Q.M.S.DORMON.M. discharged on termination of Military Service. (Authority:- T.F.Records No.298.R.E. 2 of 22.1.16 and 2.3.16.)	

O.C. 1/6TH LONDON FIELD COY, R.E.T.
CAPTAIN,

Army Form C. 2118.

WAR DIARY APPENDIX "A".

Summary of Events and Information

(Erase heading not required.)

TRANSFERS.

No. 869.Spr.BLUETT.W.H. transferred from 2/6th LONDON FIELD CO.R.E...7. 3. 16.
    2895. " HOBBS.T.W.D.   do   do
    891. " WARNE.G.H.E.   do   do
    984. " ROGERS.A.D.   do   do
    2902. " NICHOLLS.L.A.   do   do
    2940. " REID.J.   do   do
    2990. " WINNING.J.   do   do
    3015. " ANNISS.G.J.   do   do
    3016. " LAWRENCE.P.J.   do   do
    2912. " BRIERLEY.J.W.   do   do
    2942. " CUDMORE.C.E.C.   do   do
    2952. " FOSTER.W.G.   do   do
    2837. " RATHBONE.A.H.   do   do
    1118.Dvr.COFFIN.J.   do   3/4th LONDON FIELD CO.R.E.

No. 2943.Spr.WIGGINS.G.T.transferred from 2/6th LONDON FIELD CO.R.E. 14/3/16.
    2944. " REANEY.A.A.   do   do
    2996. " SOUCH.A.E.   do   do
    2997. " LAMPLOUGH.E.L.   do   do

Army Form C. 2118.

WAR DIARY APPENDIX "B"

(Erase heading not required.)

Instructions regarding War Diaries and Intelligence Summaries are contained in F. S. Regs., Part II. and the Staff Manual respectively. Title pages will be prepared in manuscript.

Place	Date	Hour	Summary of Events and Information	Remarks and references to Appendices
SUTTON VENY.			**H.S.DETAILS.**	
			No.2740.Spr.CHAPMAN.F.L. transferred to 7th PROVISIONAL FIELD CO.R.E. 15/3/16.	
			2790 " SHELTON.A. do do	
			2784 " RUSHWORTH.A.F.D. do do	
			2735 " COOPER.C.F. do do	

CONFIDENTIAL.

WAR DIARY

OF

1/6th. LONDON FIELD COMPANY, ROYAL ENGINEERS (T), 60th(LONDON) DIVISION.

FROM 1st.APRIL 1916, to 30th.APRIL 1916.

---oOo---

VOLUME V.

Army Form C. 2118.

WAR DIARY
of
INTELLIGENCE SUMMARY.

(Erase heading not required.)

Instructions regarding War Diaries and Intelligence Summaries are contained in F.S. Regs., Part II. and the Staff Manual respectively. Title pages will be prepared in manuscript.

Place	Date	Hour	Summary of Events and Information	Remarks and references to Appendices
SUTTON VENY.	1916. Apl.			
	1st.	7.30 to 8. 9.0 to 12.	Physical Drill. Section Drill and Camp Fatigues.	
	2nd.	10.45.	Church Parade.	
	3rd.	7.30) to 8.) 9.30) to 4.)	Training Carried out in accordance with Weekly Programme.	"A"
	4th.	7.30) to 8.) 9.0) to 11) 12.30 to 4.	Training carried out in accordance with Weekly Programme. Company engaged on Route March, SUTTON VENY, LONGBRIDGE DEVERILL, CROCKERTON GREEN, WARMINSTER, SUTTON VENY. (Ref.O.S.Sheet No.122 1" to 1 mile)	"A"
	5th.	7.15. 9.0 to 4.	Emergency Alarm sounded. Company paraded with Transport and reported "Ready to Move" at 7.51 a.m. Strength on parade, Officers 6. Other Ranks 140. Horses 72. Training carried out in accordance with Weekly Programme.	"A"
	6th.	7.30) to 8.) 9.0) to 4.)	The Company found Regimental Duties. Training Carried out in accordance with Weekly Programme, with the exception of Night Entrenching, which was cancelled.	"A"

Army Form C. 2118.

WAR DIARY
~~INTELLIGENCE SUMMARY~~
(Erase heading not required.)

Place	Date	Hour	Summary of Events and Information	Remarks and references to Appendices
SUTTON VENY.	1916. Apl 7th.	7.30 to 8.) 9.0. to 12)	Training carried out in accordance with Weekly Programme.	"A"
		1.0. to 4.) 6.0.	An issue of new boots made to the Company. Foot Inspection, by Section Officers.	
	8th.	7.30 to 8.) 9.0. to 12)	Training carried out in accordance with Weekly Programme.	"A"
	9th.	10.45	The Company found Regimental Duties. Church Parade.	
	10th.	7.30 to 8.) 9.0. to 4.)	Training carried out in accordance with Weekly Programme. 2nd.Lieut.C.F.BUDENBERG admitted to Military Hospital, SUTTON VENY. 2nd.Lieut.E.H.TARGETT relinquished his commission (Reference 4th.Supplement, London Gazette 31.3.16)	"B"
	11th.	7.30 to 8.) 9.0. to 3.) 6.15. 7.0. 7. to 9.	Training carried out in accordance with Weekly Programme. Brigadier-General A.W.ROPER inspected the Sappers on works at 11.30 a.m. and the Mounted Section on the Company Waggon Park at 3.0 p.m. Officers and N.C.O's attended a Lecture on the Artillery Training Map by the Adjutant. The Emergency Alarm sounded. The Company was parading with transport in readiness for a Route March and reported "Ready to Move" at 7.12 p.m. Route March;SUTTON VENY;NORTON BAVANT;SUTTON VENY.(Ref.O.S.Sheet 122 1" to 1 mile?)	"B"

Army Form C. 2118.

WAR DIARY

~~INTELLIGENCE~~ SUMMARY

(Erase heading not required.)

Instructions regarding War Diaries and Intelligence Summaries are contained in F.S. Regs. Part II. and the Staff Manual respectively. Title pages will be prepared in manuscript.

Place	Date	Hour	Summary of Events and Information	Remarks and references to Appendices
SUTTON VENY	April 11th		The promotions and appointments as shewn in Appendix "C" took effect as sdated (Authority:-60th (London) Divsl.Engineer Orders No. 85. Part 11 Para: 3 dated 11th April, 1916.)	"C".
	12th	7.30 to 4.	The Company found Regimental Duties. All available men engaged on Camp Fatigues. 40 men vaccinated.	
			HOURS OF PARADES ALTERED IN ACCORDANCE WITH :- 60th (LONDON)DIVISION ORDER No.314 DATED 12th APRIL, 1916.	
	13th	7 to 7.45) 9 to4)	Training carried out in accordance with Weekly Programme	"E".
	14th	7 to 7.45) 9 to) 3.p.m.)	Training carried out in accordance with Weekly Programme. ROUTE MARCH:- HEMDFORD MARSH, ARMINSTER COLLON, C.OCKERTON GREEN, LONGBRIDGE DEVERELL, SUTTON VENY (Ref:- O.S.Sheet 122, Scale 1" to 1 mile).	"B".
		6.0.	One case of measles reported in Hut No.20. 24 men isolated. Foot Inspection by Section Officers.	
	15th	7to4	The Company found Regimental Duties. All available men were engaged on Fatigues. 2nd.Lieut.A.H.LEE returned from Course of Mounted Duties at ALDERSHOT.	
	16th	10.30. a.m.	Church Parade.	
			Arms & Bayonets received (Authority:- A.F.G. 1099/114.)	
	17th	7 to 7.45) 9.to) 12.) 7.00) to10.30).	Training carried out in accordance with Weekly Programme.	"D".

T2134. Wt. W708—776. 500000. 4/15. Sx J. C. & S.

Army Form C. 2118.

WAR DIARY
~~INTELLIGENCE~~ SUMMARY.

(Erase heading not required.)

Instructions regarding War Diaries and Intelligence Summaries are contained in F. S. Regs., Part II. and the Staff Manual respectively. Title pages will be prepared in manuscript.

Place	Date	Hour	Summary of Events and Information	Remarks and references to Appendices.
SUTTON VENY	18th	7 to 7.45) 9 to 12.) 7.30 to10.)	The Coy. found Regimental Duties.	
	19th	7 to 7.45.) 9 to 12.0.)	Training carried out in accordance with Weekly Programme.	"D".
			Training carried out in accordance with Weekly Programme.	"D".
	20th	7 to 7.45.	Section & Cyclist Drill	
	21st	9 to 12. 6.0.	Breastworks & Task digging. Foot Inspection by Section Officers. Coy. finds Regimental duties. (Good Friday)	
		10.45 a.m.	Church parade.	
	22nd	7to 7.45) 9t•12)	Training carried out in accordance with Weekly programme.	"D".
	23rd	10.45	Church Parade.	
	24th	7to 7.45) 9 to 12.30) 2 to 3) 7.30 to10)	Training carried out in accordance with Weekly programme.	"E".

T2134. Wt. W708—776. 500000. 4/15. S&r J. C. & S.

Army Form C. 2118.

WAR DIARY

~~INTELLIGENCE~~ SUMMARY.

(Erase heading not required.)

Instructions regarding War Diaries and Intelligence Summaries are contained in F. S. Regs., Part II. and the Staff Manual respectively. Title pages will be prepared in manuscript.

Place	Date	Hour	Summary of Events and Information	Remarks and references to Appendices
SUTTON VENY	Apl 25th	7 to 7.45) 9 to 12.30) 7.30 to 10. p.m.)	Training carried out in accordance with Weekly Programme	"E".
	26th	7 to 7.45) 9 to 12.30) 2 to 3) 7.30 to 10.p.m.)	Training carried out in accordance with Weekly Programme Kit & Section Equipment Inspection. (Mounted & Dismounted).	"E".
			Training carried out in accordance with Weekly Programme.	"E".
	27th	7 to 7.45.) 9 to 12.30) 7.30 to 10 p.m.)	Coy. finds Regimental Duties.	"E".
			Training carried out in accordance with Weekly Programme.	"E".
	28th	7 to 7.45) 9 to 12.30) 6.0.	Training carried out in accordance with Weekly Programme. Foot Inspection by Section Officers.	"E".
	29th	7 to 7.45) 9 to 12	Training carried out in accordance with Weekly Programme.	"E"

T2131. Wt. W708–770. 500000. 4/15. S. J. C. & S.

Army Form C. 2118.

WAR DIARY
~~INTELLIGENCE SUMMARY~~
(Erase heading not required.)

Instructions regarding War Diaries and Intelligence Summaries are contained in F. S. Regs., Part II. and the Staff Manual respectively. Title pages will be prepared in manuscript.

Place	Date	Hour	Summary of Events and Information	Remarks and references to Appendices
SUTTON VENY.	Apl. 30th	10.45	Church Parade.	

1/6th LONDON FIELD CO. R.E.   APPENDIX "A".

PROGRAMME OF TRAINING FOR WEEK ENDING 8th APRIL, 1916.

MONDAY 3rd April.   CO. ON DUTY.

  7.30. to 8. 0.a.m.   PHYSICAL DRILL.   R.E.CAMP.   S.VENY.
  9. 0 to 9.30.a.m.   BOMBING EXERCISES.   do.   do.
  9.30. to 4. 0.p.m.   FIELD ENTRENCHMENTS.   S.V.TRENCHES.

TUESDAY 4th April.

  7.30. to 8. 0.a.m.   RIFLE EXERCISES.   R.E.CAMP.   S.VENY.
  9. 0 to 10.0.a.m.   KNOTTING & LASHING.   do.   do.
  11. 0 to 3.30.p.m.   ROUTE MARCH.

WEDNESDAY 5th April.

  7.30. to 8. 0.a.m.   RIFLE EXERCISES.   R.E.CAMP.   S.VENY.
  9. 0. to 4. 0.p.m.   FIELD ENTRENCHMENTS.   S.V.TRENCHES.

THURSDAY 6th April.   CO. ON DUTY.

  7.30. to 8. 0.a.m.   SECTION DRILL.   R.E.CAMP.   S.VENY.
  9. 0. to 12.30.p.m. DEMOLITIONS, &c.   do.   do.
  8.30. to 12.0.(Night) FIELD ENTRENCHMENTS   S.V.TRENCHES.
     p.m.

FRIDAY 7th April.

  9. 0. to 9.30.a.m.   RIFLE EXERCISES.   R.E.CAMP.   S.VENY.
  9.30. to 4. 0.p.m.   FIELD ENTRENCHMENTS, &c.   S.V.TRENCHES.
  5.30.p.m.   PAY PARADE.

SATURDAY 8th April.

  7.30. to 8. 0.a.m.   PHYSICAL DRILL.   R.E.CAMP.   S.VENY.
  9. 0. to 12.30.p.m. SECTION AND COMPANY DRILL   do.   do.
                       AND SALUTING.

DAILY:- PARTIES IN FIELD WORKS TO INSTRUCT THE INFANTRY.

MOUNTED SECTION.

DAILY.   REVEILLE..................................6 A.M.
         MORNING STABLES..........................6.30.a.m.
         MIDDAY STABLES...........................12. 0.noon.
         EVENING STABLES..........................4.30.p.m.

HALF-HOUR RIFLE EXERCISE, RIDING AND DRIVING DRILL, CARE AND FITTING OF SADDLERY AND HARNESS.

                                                      CAPTAIN,
                                            O.C. 1/6th LONDON FIELD COY. R.E.T.

1/6th LONDON FIELD CO. R.E.   APPENDIX "B".

PROGRAMME OF TRAINING FOR WEEK-ENDING 15th APRIL, 1916.

MONDAY 10th April.

7.30. to 8.0.a.m.	Physical Drill	R.E.CAMP.
9.0. to 4.0.p.m.	Pontooning (Details).	LONGLEAT PARK.
9.0. to 4.0.p.m.	Spar Bridging.	CAMP FIELD.

TUESDAY 11th April.

7.30. to 8.0.a.m.	Physical Drill & Musketry	R.E.CAMP.
9.0. to 3.0.p.m.	Earthworks, Revetting & Entanglements	S.V.TRENCHES.
6.0. to 9.0.p.m.	Route March	

WEDNESDAY 12th April.   CO.ON DUTY.

7.30. to 8.0.a.m.	Physical Drill	R.E.CAMP.
9.0. to 4.0.p.m.	Use of Explosives & Demolitions.	S.V.TRENCHES.

THURSDAY 13th April.

7.30. to 8.0.a.m.	Physical Drill	R.E.CAMP.
9.0. to 4.0.p.m.	Breastworks.	S.V.TRENCHES.

FRIDAY 14th April.

7.30. to 8.0.a.m.	Physical Drill.	R.E.CAMP.
9.0. to 4.0.p.m.	Route March & Bridging (Rations to be carried and cooked by men. Route to be selected)	

SATURDAY 15th April.   CO.ON DUTY.

7.30. to 8.0.a.m.	Kit & Rifle Inspection	R.E.CAMP.
9.0. to12.0.noon.	Co.Drill & Fatigues	do

DAILY:-   PARTIES IN FIELD WORKS TO INSTRUCT THE INFANTRY

MOUNTED SECTION.

DAILY.
- REVEILLE — — — — — — — — — — — 6.0.a.m.
- MORNING STABLES — — — — — — — — 6.30.a.m.
- MIDDAY STABLES — — — — — — — — 12.0.noon.
- EVENING STABLES — — — — — — — — 4.30.p.m.

HALF-HOUR RIFLE EXERCISE, RIDING AND DRIVING DRILL,
AND CARE AND FITTING OF SADDLERY & HARNESS

H. T. Curtis
Lieut.
for O.C. 1/6th Ld. Fd. Co. R.E.

APPENDIX "C"

PROMOTIONS.

REG.NO.	RANK AND NAME.	PROMOTED :-	Date.
1226.	Corpl. Hilborne S.C.	Actg. Serjeant.	7.4.16.
2698.	" Blizard H.A.	do.	do.
2679.	2/Cpl. Peterson W.H.	Actg. Corporal.	do.
2769.	" Weaving G.T.	do.	do.
2781.	" Hilliard H.J.	do.	do.
2761.	" Parson F.C.S.	do.	do.
2765.	" Thompson J.R.	do.	do.
2763.	L/Cpl. Nicholls W.	Actg. 2/Corpl.	do.
2772.	" Clement L.J.	do.	do.
2743.	" Quaintance W.S.	do.	do.
2783.	" Rose A.	do.	do.
2879.	" Rose J.W.	do.	do.
2744.	" Dawes H.	do.	do.
2918.	Corpl. Allingham H.E.	Actg. Serjeant.	do.
1621.	2/Cpl. Wells R.E.	Actg. Corporal.	do.

APPOINTMENTS.   Appointed.

2745. Sapper Streeter, D.G.   Lance Corporal.   do.

2764. Driver. Snee A.   do.   do.

TRANSFER.

1226. **Cpl.** Hilborne S.C.   Transferred from 2/4th London
                                     Field Coy. R.E.   7.4.16.
                                     (Authority :- T.F.Records,1652.
                                     R.E.2.d/- 10.4.16)

1/6th. LONDON FIELD CO. R.E. APPENDIX "D".

PROGRAMME OF TRAINING FOR WEEK ENDING 22nd. APRIL 1916.

MONDAY? 17th. April.

    7.0. to 7.45. Physical Drill   R.E.Camp.
    9.0. to 12 noon. Task digging and
                      Entanglements.   S.V.TRENCHES.
    8.0 p.m - 9.p.m. Night Entrenchments.   do.

TUESDAY, 18th. April. COY. FINDS REGIMENTAL DUTIES.
    7.0 to 7.45. Rifle Exercises.   R.E?CAMP.
    9.0 to 12 noon. Entrenchments.   S.V.TRENCHES.
    8.0 p.m.- 9 p.m. Night Entrenchments.   do.

WEDNESDAY, 19th. April.

    7.0 to 7.45. Bayonet Fighting.   R.E.CAMP.
    9.0 to 12 noon. Kit & Section Equipment
                     Inspection. (Mounted and
                     DIsmounted)   do.
    8.0 p.m.- 9 p.m. Night Entrenchments.   S.V.TRENCHES.

THURSDAY, 20th. April.

    7.0 to 7.45. Section & Cyclist Drill.   R.E.CAMP.
    9.0 to 12 noon. Breastworks & Task Digging.   S.V.TRENCHES.
    8.0 p.m.- 9 p.m. Night Entrenchments.   do.

FRIDAY, 21st. April. COY. FINDS REGIMENTAL DUTIES.
  (GOOD FRIDAY)
               Church Parade.
               Pay Parade.

SATURDAY. 22nd. April.

    7.0 to 7.45 Physical Drill.   R.E.CAMP.
    9.0 to 12 noon. Company Drill.   do.

DAILY.   Parties in Field Works to instruct Infantry.

         Signallers under instruction.

DAILY.   MOUNTED SECTION.
    6
    6.0 a.m.   Reveille.
    6.30 a.m.   Morning Stables.
    12. noon.   Mid-day   do.
    4.30 p.m.   Evening   do.

    Half-hour Rifle Exercise, Riding & Driving Drill,
    and care and fitting of Saddlery and Harness.

APPENDIX "E".

1/6th LONDON FIELD COMPANY. R.E.

PROGRAMME OF TRAINING FOR WEEK ENDING 29th APRIL, 1916.

MONDAY, 24th APRIL.   COMPANY FINDS REGIMENTAL DUTY.

7.0. to 7-45.	Physical Drill.	R.E.Camp.
9.0. to 12-30.	Task Digging and Revetting	S.V.Trenches.
2 p.m. to 3 p.m.	Bayonet Fighting	R.E.Camp.
7-30 p.m. to 10. p.m.	Night Entrenchments	S.V.Trenches.

TUESDAY. 25th APRIL.

7.0. to 7-45.	Rifle Exercises.	R.E.Camp.
9.0. to 12-30.	Entrenchments & Wiring.	S.V.Trenches.
7-30.p.m. to 10.p.m.	Night Entrenchments, Hand Grenades & Bombing.	do.

WEDNESDAY. 26th APRIL.

7.0. to 7-45.	Bayonet Fighting.	R.E.Camp.
9.0. to 12-30.	Kit & Section Equipment inspection.	
p.m.	(Mounted & Dismounted)	do.
2.0. to 3.0.	Bayonet Fighting & Bombing	do.
7-30.p.m. to 10.p.m.	Night Entrenchments.	S.V.Trenches.

THURSDAY. 27th APRIL.   COMPANY FINDS REGIMENTAL DUTY.

7.0. to 7-45.	Section & Cyclist drill.	R.E.Camp.
9.0. to 12-30.	Breastworks & Task digging.	S.V.Trenches.
7-30.p.m. to 10 p.m.	Night Entrenchments	do.

FRIDAY.   28th APRIL.

7.0. to 7-45.	Physical Drill.	R.E.Camp.
9.0. to 12-30.	Task Digging & Entrenchments	S.V.Trenches.
7-30 p.m. to 10 p.m.	Night Entrenchments.	do.
	PAY PARADE.	

SATURDAY.   29th APRIL.

7.0. to 7-45.	Physical Drill.	R.E.Camp.
9.0. to 12 noon	Company Drill.& Bayonet fighting.	do.

DAILY.

Parties in Field Works to instruct Infantry.

Signallers under instruction.

MOUNTED SECTION.

DAILY.

6.0.a.m.	Reveille.
6.30.a.m.	Morning Stables.
12 noon.	Mid-day do.
4.30.p.m.	Evening do.

Half-hour Rifle Exercises, Riding and Driving Drill and Care and fitting of Saddlery and Harness.

OFFICERS RIDE ON TUESDAY AND THURSDAY, 2-15 p.m. to 3-15.p.m.

CONFIDENTIAL.

WAR DIARY

OF

1/6th LONDON FIELD COMPANY, ROYAL ENGINEERS, 60th (LONDON) DIVISION.

FROM 1st MAY, 1916 to 31st MAY, 1916.

----------oOo----------

VOLUME VI.

Army Form C. 2118.

WAR DIARY

INTELLIGENCE SUMMARY.

(Erase heading not required.)

Instructions regarding War Diaries and Intelligence Summaries are contained in F.S. Regs., Part II. and the Staff Manual respectively. Title pages will be prepared in manuscript.

Place	Date	Hour	Summary of Events and Information	Remarks and references to Appendices
SUTTON VENY.	1916 May. 1st.	7.0. to 7.45. 9.0. to 12. 2.0. to 5.	Lieut.H.T.Curtis proceeded to France for a period of attachment to the British Army in the Field. Training carried out in accordance with Weekly Programme. Received intimation that 2nd.Lieut.G.F.Budenberg had been admitted to Hospital (while on Sick leave) 28.4.16.	"A". W.Y.C.
	2nd.	7.0. to 7.45. 2.0. to 12.30. 7.45 p.m. to 10.15.p.m.	Training carried out in accordance with Weekly Programme.	"A". W.Y.C.
	3rd.	7.0. to 7.45. 9.0. to 12.30. 7.45.p.m. to 10.15.p.m.	The Company Found Regimental Duties. Training carried out in accordance with Weekly Programme.	"A". W.Y.C.
	4th.	7.0.		

Army Form C. 2118.

WAR DIARY

INTELLIGENCE SUMMARY.

(Erase heading not required.)

Place	Date	Hour	Summary of Events and Information	Remarks and references to Appendices
SUTTON VENY.	4th	7.0. to 7.45.) 9.0. to 3.30.)	Training carried out in accordance with Weekly Programme.	"A". WK
	5th	7.0. to 7.45.) 9.0. to 12.30.) 2.0. to 4.0.) 5.0. to 5.30.)	Training carried out in accordance with Weekly Programme. Foot Inspection by Section Officers.	"A". WK
	6th	7.0. to 7.45.) 9.0. to 12.)	Training carried out in accordance with Weekly Programme.	"A". WK
	7th.	9.15.	Church Parade.	WK
			2nd.Lieut. W.B.Bacon commenced Course in Mounted Duties at Aldershot.	WK
			2 N.C.O's and 17 men returned to duty from Pontooning Course at Christchurch.	

Army Form C. 2118.

WAR DIARY

INTELLIGENCE SUMMARY.

(Erase heading not required.)

Instructions regarding War Diaries and Intelligence
Summaries are contained in F. S. Regs., Part II.
and the Staff Manual respectively. Title pages
will be prepared in manuscript.

Place	Date	Hour	Summary of Events and Information	Remarks and references to Appendices
SUTTON VENY.	May 8th	7.0. to 7.45.) 9.0. to 12.30) 2.0. to 5.) 7.0. to 10.30.) p.m.)	Lieut. H.W. Curtis transferred to 3/3rd London Field Company, R.E. as from 8.5.15.	"B" WJC
			Training carried out in accordance with Weekly Programme.	"B" WJC
	9th	7.0. to 7.45.) 9.0. to 12.30.) 7.45. to 10.15.) p.m.)	The Company found Regimental Duties.	"B" WJC
			Training carried out in accordance with Weekly Programme.	"B" WJC
	10th	7.0. to 7.45.) 8.30. to 5.0.) 7.45. to 10.15. p.m.)	Training carried out in accordance with Weekly Programme.	

Wt. W708—776. 500000. 4/16. Sm J. C. & S.

Army Form C. 2118.

WAR DIARY

INTELLIGENCE SUMMARY.

(Erase heading not required.)

Instructions regarding War Diaries and Intelligence
Summaries are contained in F. S. Regs., Part II.
and the Staff Manual respectively. Title pages
will be prepared in manuscript.

Place	Date	Hour	Summary of Events and Information	Remarks and references to Appendices
MUTTON VENY.	11th	7.0. to 7.45.	2 Sappers and 1 Driver transferred from 2/6th London Field Company, R.E. to 1/5th London Field Company, R.E.	"F". A/C
		9.0. to 3.30.	Training carried out in accordance with Weekly Programme.	"B" A/C
	12th	7.0. to 7.45.	The Company found Regimental Duties.	
		9.0. to 12.30. 2.0. to 4.0. 5.0. to 5.30.	Training carried out in accordance with Weekly Programme.	"B" A/C
			Foot inspection by Section Officers.	
	13th	7.0. to 7.45.		
		9.0. to 12.0.	Training carried out in accordance with Weekly Programme.	"B" A/C
	14th	9.15.	Church Parade.	

T2134. Wt. W708—778. 500000. 4/15. Sr. J. C. & S.

Army Form C. 2118.

WAR DIARY
~~INTELLIGENCE SUMMARY~~

(Erase heading not required.)

Instructions regarding War Diaries and Intelligence Summaries are contained in F. S. Regs., Part II. and the Staff Manual respectively. Title pages will be prepared in manuscript.

Place	Date	Hour	Summary of Events and Information	Remarks and references to Appendices
SUTTON VENY.	May 15th	7.0. to 7.45. 9.0. to 4.00. 8.30.p.m. to 11.0.p.m.	No.2660. Pnr.Simmons C.E. Commenced Course in Cold Shoeing at Romsey. Training carried out in accordance with Weekly Programme.	"C" WJC
	16th	7.0. to 7.45. 9.0. to 12.30. 3.0. to 4.0.	5 Sappers transferred to 7th Provisional Field Company, R.E. Training carried out in accordance with Weekly Programme.	"C" WJC "C"
	17th	7.30 to 12.30. 7.45.p.m. to 10.15.p.m.	2nd.Lieut.C.F.Budenberg discharged from Hospital, 17. 5. 16. Training carried out in accordance with Weekly Programme.	"C" WJC
	~~18th~~	7.0.	2nd.Lieut. E.H.J.Stewart attended Cookery Course at R.A.M.C.Training Centre, Sling, Bulford, 17. 5. 16. to 19.5.16.	

T2134. Wt. W708—776. 500000. 4/15. Sw J. C. & S.

Army Form C. 2118.

WAR DIARY
INTELLIGENCE SUMMARY
(Erase heading not required.)

Instructions regarding War Diaries and Intelligence Summaries are contained in F. S. Regs., Part II. and the Staff Manual respectively. Title pages will be prepared in manuscript.

Place	Date	Hour	Summary of Events and Information	Remarks and references to Appendices
SUTTON VENY	18th	7.0. to 7.45.	2nd.Lieut.C.F.Budenberg granted Sick Leave from 18.5.16. to 31.5.16.	
		9.0. to 12.30.	The Company found Regimental Duties.	
		2.0. to 3.30.	Training carried out in accordance with Weekly Programme	"C" AYC
	19th	7.0. to 7.45.	2nd.Lieut.E.H.J.Stewart returned to duty from Cookery Course, at Sling, Bulford.	
		9.0. to 4.0.	Training carried out in accordance with Weekly Programme.	
		5.0. to 5.30.	Foot inspection by Section Officers.	"C" AYC
	20th	7.0. to 7.45.		
		9.0. to 12.0.	Training carried out in accordance with Weekly Programme.	"C" AYC
	21st	9.15.	Church Parade.	

Army Form C. 2118.

WAR DIARY

INTELLIGENCE SUMMARY

(Erase heading not required.)

Instructions regarding War Diaries and Intelligence Summaries are contained in F. S. Regs., Part II. and the Staff Manual respectively. Title pages will be prepared in manuscript.

Place	Date	Hour	Summary of Events and Information	Remarks and references to Appendices
SUTTON VENY.	22nd	7.0. to 7.45.	8 Sappers transferred from 2/6th London Field Company, R.E. to 1/6th London Field Company, R.E.	"H" AYC
		9.0. to 4.0.	Training carried out in accordance with Weekly Programme.	"D" AYC
		8.30.p.m. to 11.0.p.m.		
	23rd	7.0. to 7.45.	1 N.C.O. and 2 Sappers transferred to 7th Provisional Field Coy.	"I" AYC
		9.0. to 12.30.	Training carried out in accordance with Weekly Programme	"D" AYC
		2.0. to 4.0.		
	24th		DIVISIONAL ROUTE MARCH.	"D" AYC
	25th	7.0. to 7.45.		
		9.0. to 12.30.	Training carried out in accordance with Weekly Programme.	"D" AYC
		2.0. to 4.0.		

Army Form C. 2118.

WAR DIARY
INTELLIGENCE SUMMARY
(Erase heading not required.)

Instructions regarding War Diaries and Intelligence Summaries are contained in F. S. Regs., Part II. and the Staff Manual respectively. Title pages will be prepared in manuscript.

Place	Date	Hour	Summary of Events and Information	Remarks and references to Appendices
SUTTON VENY.	May 26th	6.30.p.m.	DIVISIONAL TRENCH ATTACK. Foot Inspection by section Officers.	"D" Coy
	27th		The Company Found Regimental Duties. No.2736. Pnr.Lawford completed Course in Cold Shoeing and returned to duty.	"D" Coy
		7.0. to 7.45. 9.0. to 12.0.	Training carried out in accordance with Weekly Programme.	
	28th	9.15.	Church Parade.	
	29th	7.0. to 7.45. 9.0. to 12.0. 2.0. to 4.0.	Training carried out in accordance with Weekly Programme.	"E" Coy

T2134. Wt. W708—776. 500000. 4/15. Sir J. C. & S.

APPENDIX "A"

1/6th LONDON FIELD COMPANY. R.E.

PROGRAMME OF TRAINING FOR WEEK ENDING 6th MAY, 1916.

MONDAY, 1st MAY.

7.0. to 7-45.	Bayonet Fighting.	R.E.CAMP.
9.0. to 12-30.	Field Works.	S.V.TRENCHES.
2.0. to 5.0.	Ditto.	do.

TUESDAY, 2nd. MAY.

7.0. to 7-45.	Rifle Exercises.	R.E.CAMP.
9.0. to 12-30.	Demolitions.	S.V.TRENCHES.
7-45 p.m. to 10-15.	Revetting.	do.

WEDNESDAY, 3rd. MAY. COMPANY FINDS REGIMENTAL DUTIES.

7.0. to 7-45.	Section Drill.	R.E.CAMP.
9.0. to 12-30.	Demolitions.	S.V.TRENCHES.
7-45 p.m. to 10-15.	Field Works.	do.

THURSDAY, 4th MAY.

7.0. to 7-45.	Bayonet Fighting.	R.E.CAMP.
9.0. to 3-30.	Route March & Pontooning.	LONGLEAT PARK.

FRIDAY, 5th MAY.

7.0. to 7-45.	Rifle Exercises.	R.E.CAMP.
9.0. to 12-30.	Revetting & Entrenchments.	S.V.TRENCHES.
2.0. to 4.0.	Demolitions.	do.
5.0.	PAY PARADE.	R.E.CAMP.

SATURDAY, 6th MAY. COMPANY FINDS REGIMENTAL DUTIES.

7.0. to 7-45.	Physical Drill.	R.E.CAMP.
9.0. to 12.0.	Company Drill & Bayonet Fighting.	do.

DAILY.

Parties in Field Works to instruct Infantry.

MOUNTED SECTION.

DAILY.

6. 0.a.m.	Reveille.
6.30.a.m.	Morning Stables.
12.0.noon.	Mid-day Stables.
4.30.p.m.	Evening do.

Half hour Rifle Exercises, Riding and Driving Drill and care and fitting of Saddlery & Harness.

W.H. Culson CAPTAIN.
O.C. 1/6th LONDON FIELD COY. R.E.T.

Army Form C. 2118.

WAR DIARY

~~INTELLIGENCE SUMMARY.~~

(Erase heading not required.)

Instructions regarding War Diaries and Intelligence Summaries are contained in F. S. Regs., Part II. and the Staff Manual respectively. Title pages will be prepared in manuscript.

Place	Date	Hour	Summary of Events and Information	Remarks and references to Appendices
SUTTON VENY.	May 30th	7.0. to 9.0.	The Company found Regimental duties.	
		10.0. 10.0. to 12.0. 2.0. p 4.0.	Inspection by G.O.C. ~~Training carried out in accordance with Weekly Programme.~~	"E" SMC
	31st		Royal Review. 2nd.Lieut. C.F.Budenberg returned to duty from Sick Leave.	SMC

CAPTAIN.
O.C. 1/6th LONDON FIELD COY. R.E.T.

APPENDIX "B".

1/6th LONDON FIELD COMPANY, R.E.

PROGRAMME OF TRAINING FOR WEEK ENDING 13th MAY, 1916.

MONDAY, 8th MAY.

7.0. to 7.45.	Bayonet Fighting.		R.E.CAMP.
9.0. to 12.30.	Spar Bridging.		HINDFORD MARSH.
2.0. to 5.0.	ditto.		ditto.
7.0. to 10.30.	Field Works.		S.V. TRENCHES.

TUESDAY, 9th MAY.   COMPANY FINDS REGIMENTAL DUTIES.

7.0. to 7.45.	Rifle Exercises.	R.E.CAMP.
9.0. to 12.30.	Demolitions.	S.V. TRENCHES.
7.45.p.m. to 10.15.p.m.	Revetting.	ditto.

WEDNESDAY, 10th MAY.

7.0. to 7.45.	Section Drill.	R.E.CAMP.
8.30. to 5.0.	Field Works.	S.V. TRENCHES.
7.45.p.m. to 10.15.p.m.	Wire Entanglements and Demolitions.	Ditto.

THURSDAY, 11th MAY.

7.0. to 7.45.	Bayonet Fighting.	R.E.CAMP.
9.0. to 3.30.	Route March and Pontooning.	LONGLEAT PARK.

FRIDAY, 12th MAY.   COMPANY FINDS REGIMENTAL DUTIES.

7.0. to 7.45.	Rifle Exercises.	R.E.CAMP.
9.0. to 12.30.	Revetting.	S.V. TRENCHES.
2.0. to 4.0.	Spar Bridging.	
5.0.	PAY PARADE.	

SATURDAY, 13th MAY.

7.0. to 7.45.	Physical Drill.	R.E.CAMP.
9.0. to 12.0.	Company Drill and Bayonet Fighting.	Ditto.

MOUNTED SECTION.

DAILY.

6. 0.a.m..................Reveille.
6.30.a.m..................Morning Stables.
12 noon...................Mid-day do.
4.30.p.m..................Evening do.

Half hour Rifle Exercises, Riding and Driving Drill and care and fitting of Saddlery and Harness.

[signature] CAPTAIN,
O.C. 1/6th LONDON FIELD COY. R.E.T.

APPENDIX "C"

1/6th LONDON FIELD COMPANY, R.E.

PROGRAMME OF TRAINING FOR WEEK ENDING 20th MAY, 1916.

MONDAY, 15th MAY.   COMPANY FINDS REGIMENTAL DUTIES.

7.0.	to	7.45.	Bayonet Fighting.	R.E.CAMP.
9.0.	to	4.0.	Pontooning.	LONGLEAT PARK.
8.30.	to	11.0.	Field Works & Wire	
p.m.		p.m.	Entanglements.	S.V.TRENCHES.

TUESDAY, 16th MAY.

7.0.	to	7.45.	Rifle Exercises.	R.E.CAMP.
9.0.	to	12.30.	Field Works & Demolitions.	S.V.TRENCHES.
3.0.	to	4.0.	Medical Inspection.	R.E.CAMP.

WEDNESDAY, 17th MAY.

7.30.	to	12.30.	Route March.	
7.45.p.m.	to	10.15.p.m.	Wire Entanglements and Demolitions.	S.V.TRENCHES.

THURSDAY, 18th MAY.   COMPANY FINDS REGIMENTAL DUTIES.

7.0.	to	7.45.	Squad Drill without Arms.	R.E.CAMP.
9.0.	to	12.30.	Demolitions.	do.
2.0.	to	3.30.	Wire Entanglements. Extension of Working parties.	do.

FRIDAY, 19th MAY.

7.0.	to	7.45.	Rifle Exercises.	R.E.CAMP.
9.0.	to	4.0.	Spar Bridging.(Knotting and Splicing)	do.
		5.0.	Pay Parade.	do.

SATURDAY, 20th MAY.

7.0.	to	7.45.	Physical Drill.	R.E.CAMP.
9.0.	to	12.0.	Company Drill and Bayonet fighting.	do.

MOUNTED SECTION.

DAILY.

6.0.a.m.	Reveille.
6.30.a.m.	Morning Stables.
12 noon	Mid-day do.
4.30.p.m.	Evening do.

Half hour Rifle Exercises and Squad Drill, Riding and Driving Drill and care and fitting of Saddlery & Harness.

[signature] CAPTAIN,
O.C. 1/6th LONDON FIELD COY. R.E.T.

1/6th. London Field Company, R.E. APPENDIX "D"

PROGRAMME OF TRAINING FOR WEEK ENDING 27th. MAY 1916.

MONDAY 22nd. May.

7.0 to 7.45.	Bayonet Fighting and Rifle Exercises	R.E.CAMP.
9.0 to 4.0.	Pontooning.	LONGLEAT PK.
8.30 to 11.0.	Entanglements and Obstacles.	S.V.TRENCHES.

TUESDAY 23rd. May.

7.0 to 7.45.	Bayonet Fighting and Rifle Exercises.	R.E.CAMP.
9.0 to 12.30.	Wire Entanglements and Demolitions.	S.V.TRENCHES.
2.0 to 4.0.	Packing and Unpacking Tool-carts, Packs etc., and Setting-up Pumps, Troughs etc.	R.E.CAMP.

WEDNESDAY 24th. May. — COMPANY FINDS REGIMENTAL DUTIES.

DIVISIONAL ROUTE MARCH.

THURSDAY 25th. May.

7.0 to 7.45	Rifle Exercises.	R.E.CAMP.
9.0 to 12.30.	Spar Bridging.	do.
2.0 to 4.0.	Wire Entanglements and Demolitions, Lecture on Road Reconnaisance etc.	S.V.TRENCHES.

FRIDAY 26th. May.

DIVISIONAL TRENCH ATTACK.

SATURDAY 27th. May. — COMPANY FINDS REGIMENTAL DUTIES.

7.0 to 7.45.	Physical Training.	R.E.Camp.
9.0 to 12.0	Company and Section Drill and Bayonet Fighting.	do.

MOUNTED SECTION.

DAILY.

6.0 a.m............Reveille.
6.30 a.m...........Morning Stables.
12 noon............Mid-day Stables.
4.30 p.m...........Evening Stables.

Half-hour Rifle Exercises and Squad Drill, Riding and Driving Drill and care and fitting of Saddlery and Harness.

Infantry Instruction Parties as required.

1/6th. London Field Coy. R.E.   APPENDIX "E"

PROGRAMME OF TRAINING FOR WEEK COMMENCING 29th. MAY 1916.

Monday 29th.
   7. to 7.45 a.m.   Physical Drill and Gas Helmet Instn.   R.E.CAMP.
   9. to 12.0.   Company Drill (Drivers to attend)   do.
   2.0 to 4.0.   Wire Entanglements and Extension of
        Working Parties.   S.V.TRENCHES.

Tuesday 30th.   Company Finds Regimental Duties.
   7. to 7.45 a.m.   Bayonet Fighting and Gas Helmet Instn.   R.E.CAMP.
   9.0 to 10.0.   Company Drill (Drivers to attend)   do.
   10.0 to 12.0.   O.R.E's Parade.   do.
   2.0 to 4.0.   Gas Helmet Instruction and Wire
        Entanglements.   S.V.TRENCHES.

Wednesday 31st.   INSPECTION.

Thursday June 1st.
   7. to 7.45 a.m.   Rifle Exercises, Bayonet Fighting
        and Gas Helmet Instruction.   R.E.CAMP.
   9.1 to 10.0   Complete Section Inspection by
        Officers i/c Sections.   do.
   11.0 to 3.0.   Route March.   ROUTE TO BE SELECTED

Friday 2nd.   Company Finds Regimental Duties.
   7. to 7.45 a.m.   Section Drill and Gas Helmet Instn.   R.E.CAMP.
   9.0 to 12.30   Spar Bridging.   do.
   2.0. to 4.0.   Demolitions.   S.V.TRENCHES.
   5.0.   Pay Parade.

Saturday 3rd.
   7. to 7.45 a.m.   Physical Training.   R.E.CAMP.
   9. to 10.30.   Company Inspection by O.C.   do.
   11.0 to 12.0.   Company Drill and Saluting.   do.

   DAILY.   N.C.O's Drill and Duties Class.   7.0 to 8.0 a.m.

   MOUNTED SECTION.
   Morning Stables............ 6.30.
   Mid-day Stables............ 12.0.
   Evening Stables............ 4.30.
DAILY. Half-hour Rifle Exercises, Half-hour Riding and
   Driving Drill and Care and Fitting of Saddlery
   and Harness.

INFANTRY WORKING PARTIES AS REQUIRED.

R.E.Camp,
Sutton Veny,

APPENDIX "F".

TRANSFERS.

2950.	Spr.	Gale A.E.	)
			)
3002.	"	Grimsley J.	) Transferred from 2/6th London Field
			) Company, R.E. 11.5.15.
3076.	"	Uncles H.R.H.	)

[signature] CAPTAIN,
O.C. 1/6th LONDON FIELD COY. R.E., T.

APPENDIX "G".

TRANSFERS.

2754.	Spr. Murton C.M.	Transferred to 7th Provisional Field Company, R.E. Weeley. (Authority T.F.Records 1943. R.E.2. 29.4.16.)	16. 5. 16.
2693.	Spr. Allardice G.H.	Transferred to 7th Provisional Field Company, R.E. Weeley. (Authority T.F.Records 2099. R.E.2. 8.5.16.)	16. 5. 16.
2799.	" Everard F.C.	ditto.	
2708.	Pnr. Newham F.E.	ditto.	
2940.	Spr. Reid J.	ditto.	

D.F.Colson CAPT
O.C. 1/6th LONDON FIELD COY. R.E.

APPENDIX "H".

TRANSFERS.

2868.	Spr.	Hall J.W.	Transferred from 2/6th London Fld.Coy.R.E. 22.5.16.
2826.	"	Kemp S.J.	ditto.
2941.	"	Clark G.F.	ditto.
3291.	"	Gilham F.H.	ditto.
2892.	"	Rose L.	ditto.
2899.	"	Carter W.H.	ditto.
3008.	"	Hutton R.A.	ditto.
3003.	"	Fisher F.	ditto.

D.J.Colson CAPTAIN,
O.C. 1/6th LONDON FIELD COY. R.E.T.

APPENDIX "I".

TRANSFERS.

2763. 2/Cpl. Nicholls W.   Transferred to 7th Provisional Field
                             Company, R.E.   23.5.16.
                             (Authority - T.F.Records.2203.R.E.
                              2. 15.5.16.)

2669. Spr.Riches W.   ditto.

2876. " Byway J.W.   ditto.

signature CAPTAIN
O.C. 1/6th LONDON FIELD COY. R.E.

Confidential.

War Diary.

of

Royal Engineers, 60th (London) Division.

16th London Field Company.

From 1st June 1916. to 22nd June 96.

Volume VII

RECEIVED BY
2 4 JUN 1916
T.F. RECORDS, LONDON

Army Form C. 2118.

WAR DIARY
or
INTELLIGENCE SUMMARY
(Erase heading not required.)

Instructions regarding War Diaries and Intelligence Summaries are contained in F. S. Regs., Part II. and the Staff Manual respectively. Title Pages will be prepared in manuscript.

Place	Date	Hour	Summary of Events and Information	Remarks and references to Appendices
SUTTON VENY.	JUNE 1st.	7.0. to 7.45.) 9.0. to 12.0.) 2.0. to 4.0.)	Training carried out in accordance with Weekly Programme	"A" K.Y.C
			2nd.Lieut. W.H.Lee granted leave from 1.6.16. to 4.6.16.	
			2nd.Lieut. B.F. Nell do do do.	
			The promotions and appointments as shown in appendix "D" took effect as dated (Ref:60th (London) Divsl.Engineers Orders No.137 d/- 8.6.16.)	"D" K.Y.C
	2nd.	7.0. to 7.45.) 9.0. to 12.30.) 2.0. to 4.0.) 5.30.	Training carried out in accordance with Weekly Programme.	"A" K.Y.C
			Foot inspection by Section Officers.	
			7 Sappers and 3 Drivers transferred from 2/6th London Field Company, R.E. to 1/6th London Field Company, R.E.	"E" K.Y.C

2449 Wt. W14957/M90 750,000 1/16 J.B.C. & A. Forms/C.2118/12.

Army Form C. 2118.

WAR DIARY
or
INTELLIGENCE SUMMARY

(Erase heading not required.)

Instructions regarding War Diaries and Intelligence Summaries are contained in F. S. Regs., Part II. and the Staff Manual respectively. Title Pages will be prepared in manuscript.

Place	Date	Hour	Summary of Events and Information	Remarks and references to Appendices
SUTTON VENY.	June 3rd.	7.0. to 7.45. 9.0. to 10.30. 11.0. to 12.0.	Training carried out in accordance with Weekly Programme.	FMC
	4th	9.15	Church Parade.	
	5th	7.0. to 7.45. 9.0. to 12.0. 2.0. to 4.0.	The Company found Regimental Duties. Training carried out in accordance with Weekly Programme. Capt.H.D.Steers granted leave to 8. 6. 16. 2nd.Lieut.W.B.Bacon granted leave to 8. 6. 16. 2nd.Lieut.A.H.Lee granted leave to 8. 6. 16. 2nd.Lieut.C.F.Budenberg granted Sick Leave to 5. 7. 16.	FMC
	6th	7.0. to 7.45. 9.0. to 4.0.	Training carried out in accordance with Weekly Programme.	FMC

2449 Wt. W14957/Mgo 750,000 1/16 J.B.C. & A. Forms/C.2118/12.

Army Form C. 2118.

WAR DIARY
or
INTELLIGENCE SUMMARY

(Erase heading not required.)

Instructions regarding War Diaries and Intelligence Summaries are contained in F. S. Regs., Part II. and the Staff Manual respectively. Title Pages will be prepared in manuscript.

Place	Date	Hour	Summary of Events and Information	Remarks and references to Appendices
SUTTON VENY.	June 6th		No. 2736. Pnr. Lawford W. passed Course in Cold Shoeing at School of Farriery, Romsey.	
	7th	7.0. to 7.45. 9.0. to 12.0. 2.0. to 4.0.	) Training carried out in accordance with Weekly Programme)))))	"B"4C
	8th	7.0. to 7.45. 9.0. to 12.0. 2.0. to 4.0.	) Company found Regimental Duties.) Training carried out in accordance with Weekly Programme)))	"B"4C
			No. 2661. Pnr. Rogers G.W. returned to duty from Course in Cold Shoeing at Romsey in which he passed a Course.	
	9th	7.0. to 7.45. 9.0. to 12.0. 3.0. to 5.30.	) Training carried out in accordance with Weekly Programme)))) Foot Inspection by Section OFFICERS.	"B"4C

2449 Wt. W14957/M90 750,000 1/16 J.B.C. & A. Forms/C.2118/12.

Army Form C. 2118.

WAR DIARY
or
INTELLIGENCE SUMMARY

(Erase heading not required.)

Instructions regarding War Diaries and Intelligence Summaries are contained in F. S. Regs., Part II. and the Staff Manual respectively. Title Pages will be prepared in manuscript.

Place	Date	Hour	Summary of Events and Information	Remarks and references to Appendices
SUTTON VENY.	9th		Capt. D.F.Colson granted leave to 12. 6. 16. 2nd.Lieut. B.H.J Stewart granted leave to 12. 6. 16. 2nd.Lieut. G.W.Bacon granted leave to 12. 6. 16.	GWC
	10th	7.0. to 7.45.	Physical Training.	
		9.0 to 12.0.	Section Drill. Saluting Drill.	
			2nd.lieut.C F.Budenberg transferred to 6/2nd.London Divnl Engineers. (Authority :- Hd. Qr.London Dis. G.R. I.D.63/22 of 10.6.16.)	
	11th	9.15.	Church Parade. The Company found Regimental Duties.	
	12th	7.0. to 7.45. 9.0 to 4.0.	)) Training carried out in accordance with Weekly Programme.))	GWC
	13th	7.0. to 7.45. 9.0 to 3.0.	)) Training carried out in accordance with Weekly Programme.))	GWC

Army Form C. 2118.

WAR DIARY
or
INTELLIGENCE SUMMARY

(Erase heading not required.)

Instructions regarding War Diaries and Intelligence Summaries are contained in F. S. Regs., Part II. and the Staff Manual respectively. Title Pages will be prepared in manuscript.

Place	Date	Hour	Summary of Events and Information	Remarks and references to Appendices
SUNDON T.N.	June 14th	7.0. to 7.45. 9.0. to 12.30. 2.0. to 4.0.	The Company found Regimental Duties. Training carried out in accordance with Weekly Programme.	"g" XYC
	15th	7.0. to 7.45. 9.0. to 12.30. 2.0. to 4.0.	Training carried out in accordance with Weekly Programme. Captain H.D. Steers proceeded to France with Advance Party. Home Service Details. 3 Sappers transferred to 76th Provisional Field Coy. R.E.	"g" XYC "E" "g" XYC
	16th	7.0. to 7.45. 9.0. to 12.30. 2.0. to 4.0.	Training carried out in accordance with Weekly Programme	

2449 Wt. W14957/M90 750,000 1/16 J.B.C. & A. Forms/C.2118/12.

Army Form C. 2118.

WAR DIARY
or
INTELLIGENCE SUMMARY

(Erase heading not required.)

Instructions regarding War Diaries and Intelligence Summaries are contained in F.S. Regs, Part II. and the Staff Manual respectively. Title Pages will be prepared in manuscript.

Place	Date	Hour	Summary of Events and Information	Remarks and references to Appendices
HUTTON	June 16th		Home Service Details. 1 N.C.O. transferred to 7th Provisional Field Coy R.E.	"g" WC
	17th		No.2809.Spr.Harrison E.H. re-enlisted in Royal Flying Corps. Received intimation that the 7 days Programme of work before proceeding overseas would commence on the 17th inst.	" " WC
	18th		Inspection of Officers, Men, Transport and everything to be taken overseas, (in accordance with Ad.Lr.Divsl.letter No.A/3553. 20.5.16.)	WC
			Boards of Survey held on Clothing. Condemned clothing surveyed by contractor and sold to him. Clothing still serviceable was disinfected and returned to depots. Equipment ledger account closed and all surplus equipment returned to O.C Warminster and new clothing to A.O.D.Southampton.	" WC " " " "
X	19th		All personal private property of Officers and men collected and removed from Hutments. Returned all stores received for instruction and surplus to mobilization requirements Peace stores, etc. to Ordnance, Warminster. All Hutments and fixtures inspected.	" WC " "
	20th		No.2660.Pnr.Simmons E.C.returned to duty from Course in Cold Shoeing. Inspection of Gas Helmets,Field Dressings,Identity Discs, etc.	" WC
	21st		Issue of Pay Books.	" WC
	22nd		Bed Boards and Trestles, and tables and trestles stacked and piled ready for counting, also all other barrack stores. All Hutments thoroughly scrubbed out with Creosote; all rubbish burnt and buried. 1 N.C.O. 1 Sapper and 1 Driver discharged permanently unfit for Military Service. All blankets got ready for return by O.C. Details to O.i/c.Barracks.	"H" WC " WC
X	19th		General parade of all ranks,fully equipped; during inspection all private personal effects surplus left from previous inspection destroyed. 2nd.Lieut.G**ॼ**.W.BACON appointed O.i/c Details of 2/4th. 3/3rd. & 1/6th FieldCoys. & Headqrs. 60th LONDON DIVSL.ENGINEERS.	WC

Army Form C. 2118.

WAR DIARY
or
INTELLIGENCE SUMMARY

(Erase heading not required.)

Instructions regarding War Diaries and Intelligence Summaries are contained in F. S. Regs., Part II. and the Staff Manual respectively. Title Pages will be prepared in manuscript.

Place	Date	Hour	Summary of Events and Information	Remarks and references to Appendices
SUTTON VENY.	June 22nd.		Pay accounts closed. The promotions and appointments as shown in appendix "H" took effect as dated. (Ref. London Gazette, 20/6/16.)	"H"

2449 Wt. W14957/M90 750,000 1/16 J.B.C. & A. Forms/C.2118/12

APPENDIX "A"

1/6th. London Field Coy. R.E.

PROGRAMME OF TRAINING FOR WEEK COMMENCING 29th. MAY 1916.

Monday 29th.
7. to 7.45 a.m.	Physical Drill and Gas Helmet Instn.	R.E.CAMP.
8. to 12.0.	Company Drill (Drivers to attend)	do.
2.0 to 4.0.	Wire Entanglements and Extension of Working Parties.	S.V.TRENCHES.

Tuesday 30th. Company Finds Regimental Duties.
7. to 7.45 a.m.	Bayonet Fighting and Gas Helmet Instn.	R.E.CAMP.
9.0 to 10.0.	Company Drill (Drivers to attend)	do.
10.0 to 11.0.	O.R.E's Parade.	do.
2.0 to 4.0.	Gas Helmet Instruction and Wire Entanglements.	S.V.TRENCHES.

Wednesday 31st.
INSPECTION.

Thursday June 1st.
7. to 7.45 a.m.	Rifle Exercises, Bayonet Fighting and Gas Helmet Instruction.	R.E.CAMP.
9. to 10.0	Complete Section Inspection by Officers i/c Sections.	do.
11.0 to 2.0.	Route March.	ROUTE TO BE SELECTED.

Friday 2nd. Company Finds Regimental Duties.
7. to 7.45 a.m.	Section Drill and Gas Helmet Instn.	R.E.CAMP.
9.0 to 12.30	Spar Bridging.	do.
2.0. to 4.0.	Demolitions.	S.V.TRENCHES.
5.0.	Pay Parade.	

Saturday 3rd.
7. to 7.45 a.m.	Physical Training.	R.E.CAMP.
9. to 10.30.	Company Inspection by O.C.	do.
11.0 to 12.0.	Company Drill and Saluting.	do.

DAILY.   N.C.O's Drill and Duties Class.   7.0 to 8.0 p.m.

MOUNTED SECTION.
Morning Stables............ 6.30.
Mid-day Stables............ 12.0.
Evening Stables............ 4.0.

DAILY. Half hour Rifle Exercises, Half-hour Riding and Driving Drill and Care and Fitting of Saddlery and Harness.

INFANTRY WORKING PARTIES AS REQUIRED.

R.E.Camp,
Sutton Veny.

W.Y.Collins Capt.
O.C. 1/6 London Field Coy. R.E.

APPENDIX "B"

1/6th LONDON FIELD COY. R.E.

PROGRAMME OF TRAINING FOR WEEK-COMMENCING JUNE 5th, 1916.

Monday June 5th. COMPANY FINDS REGIMENTAL DUTIES.
- 7. 0. to 7. 45. a.m. Rifle Exercises R.E.CAMP.
- 9. 0. to 12. 0. noon. Wire Entanglements & Extension of Working Parties S.V.TRENCHES.
- 2. 0. to 4. 0. p.m. Demolitions. do.

Tuesday June 6th.
- 7. 0. to 7. 45. a.m. Bayonet Fighting & Section Drill. R.E.CAMP.
- 9. 0. to 4. 0. p.m. Pontoon Bridging. LONGLEAT PARK.

Wednesday June 7th.
- 7. 0. to 7. 45. a.m. Physical Training. R.E.CAMP.
- 9. 0. to 12. 0. noon. Field Works. S.V.TRENCHES.
- 2. 0. to 4. 0. p.m. Practice with Field Instruments. do.

Thursday June 8th. COMPANY FINDS REGIMENTAL DUTIES.
- 7. 0. to 7. 45. a.m. Rifle Exercises. R.E.TRENCHES.
- 9. 0. to 12. 0. noon. Demolitions. S.V.TRENCHES.
- 2. 0. to 4. 0. p.m. Field Works. do.

Friday June 9th.
- 7. 0. to 7. 45. a.m. Bayonet Fighting. R.E.CAMP.
- 9. 0. to 3. 0. p.m. Route March (Route to be selected).

DAILY:- N.C.Os. Drill & Duties Class. 7 to 8. a.m.

MOUNTED SECTION.

- MORNING STABLES - - - 6. 30. a.m.
- MIDDAY " - - - 12. 0. noon.
- EVENING " - - - 5. 0. p.m.

DAILY:- Half-hour Rifle Exercises, Half-hour Riding and Driving Drill and Care and Fitting of Saddlery and Harness.

INFANTRY WORKING PARTIES AS REQUIRED.

R.E.Camp,
SUTTON VENY

[signed]
1/6 London Field Coy. R.E.
Capt.

APPENDIX "C."

1/6th LONDON FIELD COMPANY, R.E.

PROGRAMME OF TRAINING FOR WEEK COMMENCING JUNE 12th, 1916.

MONDAY, JUNE 12th.

7.0.	to	7.45.	Bayonet Fighting and Gas Helmet Instruction.	R.E. CAMP.
9.0.	to	4.0.	Pontoon Bridging.	LONGLEAT PARK.

TUESDAY, JUNE 13th.

7.0.	to	7.45.	Rifle & Bombing Exercises and Gas Helmet Instruction.	R.E. CAMP.
9.0.	to	3.0.	Route March and Reconnaisance. (Route to be selected) During this anti gas helmets will be put on.	

WEDNESDAY, JUNE 14th. COMPANY FINDS REGIMENTAL DUTIES.

7.0.	to	7.45.	Physical Training and Gas Helmet Instruction.	R.E. CAMP.
9.0.	to	12.30.	Field Works.	S.V. TRENCHES.
2.0.	to	4.0.	Demolitions.	do.

THURSDAY, JUNE 15th.

7.0.	to	7.45.	Section Drill and Gas Helmet Instruction.	R.E. CAMP.
9.0.	to	12.30.	Entanglements and Obstacles.	S.V. TRENCHES.
2.0.	to	4.0.	Bombing (live bombs)	BOMBING GROUND.

FRIDAY, JUNE 16th.

7.0.	to	7.45.	Rifle and Bombing Exercises and Gas Helmet Instruction.	R.E. CAMP.
9.0.	to	12.30.	Knots, Lashings & Splicing.	do.
2.0.	to	4.0.	Spar Bridging. Pay Parade.	do. do.

SATURDAY, June 17th. COMPANY FINDS REGIMENTAL DUTIES.

7.0.	to	7.45.	Bayonet Fighting & Gas Helmet Instruction.
9.0.	to	10.0.	Section Drill.
10.0.	to	11.30.	Company Drill.
11.30.	to	12.0.	Saluting Drill.

MOUNTED SECTION.
Morning Stables..........6.30.a.m.
Midday   "   ....12 noon.
Evening   "   ....5.0.p.m.

Daily :- Half-hour Rifle Exercises, Half-hour Riding and Driving Drill and care and fitting of Saddlery and Harness.

PARTIES FOR DUGOUT CONSTRUCTION.

Junior N.C.O's and Sappers Drill and Duties Class daily.
Parties for instructing Pioneer Battalion in Wire Entanglements.

DURING THIS WEEK ALL RANKS WHO HAVE NOT ALREADY DONE SO MUST COMPLETE THEIR GENERAL MUSKETRY COURSE.

R.Y. Cohen
CAPTAIN,
O.C. 1/6th LONDON FIELD COY. R.E.,T.

1/6 London 2 Army Coy

WAR DIARY

INTELLIGENCE SUMMARY

(Erase heading not required.)

Army Form C. 2118

Instructions regarding War Diaries and Intelligence Summaries are contained in F.S. Regs., Part II. and the Staff Manual respectively. Title Pages. will be prepared in manuscript.

Place	Date	Hour	Summary of Events and Information	Remarks and references to Appendices
Sutton Veny	23/6/16	2.25pm	Right Half-Coy, 3 Officers, 108 other ranks, 46 Horses, 10 Vehicles, 16 Bicycles entrained at WARMINSTER.	
do	do	3.45pm	Left Half-Coy 3 Officers, 103 other ranks, 33 Horses, 9 Vehicles, 17 Bicycles, do.	
SOUTHAMPTON	do	8.0pm	Whole Company embarked	
HAVRE	24/6/16	7.0 am	Company disembarked & proceeded to Docks Rest Camp.	
do	do	2.0 pm	Received order to entrain on 25/6/16	
do	25/6/16	12.30 pm	Company entrained at POINT 6.	
ST. POL	26/6/16	5.30 am	Company detrained.	
	do	7.0 am	Company moved off. Arrived HAUTE-CÔTE at 9.30 am. O.C. Coy reported to 180 Bgde HQrs.	
HAUTE-COTE	27/6/16	3.0 am	Received orders from 180 Bde HQrs to prepare to move about noon.	
do	do	12.30 pm	Marched out. Arrived & billeted Coy at Fm DOFFINE 8.0 pm.	
Fm DOFFINE	28/6/16	12 noon	Coy, less Transport (left in charge of 2 Lt. W.H. LEE) marched out. Arrived at MONT-ST. ELOY 6 pm. O.C. Coy reported to 152 Bde HQrs.	
MONT ST ELOY	29/6/16	9 am	Fatigues, construction of Cook house, food store, office & latrines.	
		1.15 pm	2/Lt. R.B. TAYLOR reported for duty from 1/3rd Lond. R.E.	
do	30/6/16	10 am	Rifle inspection. Capt. D.F. Colson promoted Temp. Major, dated 1.5.16 (London Gazette 23/6/16)	
		11 am	Major D.F. COLSON departed to take command of 2/4 Lond. R.E.	

To be rendered to Officers i/c Records for transmission to the War Office.   Army Form B. 158.

CAVALRY, ARTILLERY and INFANTRY only.

Regiment, etc., or Depot 16th London Field Co RE T
Station Mont St Eloy
Date 30th June 1916

LIST OF OFFICERS.

*Married or Single	Officers doing duty with the Unit NAME	Date of being taken on the strength of the Unit†	Stations (if on Detachment)
	Lieut.-Colonel—		
	Majors—		
	Captains—		
S.	H. D. Steers	27. 2. 16.	
S.	C B Taylor	29. 6. 16	
	Lieutenants—		
M	W B Bacon	12. 7. 15	
M	B. T. Nell	21. 7. 15	
	2nd Lieutenants		
S	E. A. J Stewart	14. 8. 15	
S	W. H. Lee	19. 10. 15	
S	A H Lee	24. 10. 15	
	Adjutant—		
	Quartermaster—		
	Riding Master—		
	WARRANT OFFICERS.		
	Master Gunner—		
M	Serjeant-Major— F. R Martin	21. 7. 15	
	Bandmaster—		

OFFICERS ATTACHED.
(Including Special Reserve and Territorial Force Officers. Authority to be quoted.)

Rank	Name	Corps	Authority	Date of joining

* The letter "M" or "S" is to be placed before the names of Officers.
† For Units of Royal Artillery, Depots of all Arms and Special Reserve Units.
NOTE.—The word "Sick" to be inserted against the names of all Officers who are on the Sick List, and the words "Assistant Adjutant," "Instructor of Gunnery," &c., against the name of an Officer holding such appointment.

Officers absent on duty.
(Exclusive of seconded Officers, but including Officers posted and not joined.)

Married or Single	Rank and Name	On what duty, at what station, from what time

Officers and Warrant Officers absent with Leave.

Rank and Name	By whose permission, and date of order	On what account	From what time	To what time

Officers and Warrant Officers who have *joined* during the preceding month, showing whether from leave of absence, on appointment, &c.

Rank and Name	Date and cause
Capt C B Taylor	Transferred from 1/3rd Lon. Field Co. R.E. 29.6.16

Officers and Warrant Officers who have *quitted* during the preceding month, showing whether on leave of absence, removal, death, &c.

Rank and Name	Date and cause
Capt F.T. Colson	Transferred to 2/1st Lon. Field Co R.E. 30.6.16

Officers absent without leave.

Rank and Name	Since what time

CAPTAIN, Commanding.
O.C. 1/6th LONDON FIELD COY. R.E.,T.

WARDIARY
INTELLIGENCE SUMMARY
(Erase heading not required.)

Army Form C. 2118

Instructions regarding War Diaries and Intelligence Summaries are contained in F. S. Regs., Part II. and the Staff Manual respectively. Title Pages will be prepared in manuscript.

Place	Date	Hour	Summary of Events and Information	Remarks and references to Appendices
MONT ST ELOY	30.6.16	9.30pm	Right Half-Coy, under Lieut. W.B. BACON proceeded to trenches for work with 2/2nd Highland Field Coy R.E. in Left Sect, under 152nd Brigade.	
			Left Half-Coy, under Lieut. B.F. NELL proceeded to EMPIRE REDOUBT for work on Strong points under C.E. XVII Corps.	
	1.7.16		Work continued. No 2990 Spr WINNING T. evacuated to 23rd Field Clearing Stn. (Rheumatism)	
	2.7.16		Do	
	6.7.16		Do	
	7.7.16	9 p.m.	2/Lt E.H.J. STEWART (relieved by 2/Lt W.H. LEE) proceeded from trenches to take charge of transport at FERME DOFFINE.	
		8 a.m.	No 2821 Dr CLOWES G.E. admitted 2/3rd Field Ambulance & transferred to No 12 Stat Hospital.	
			No 3293 Spr TURVEY F.W. reported to O/c light Railway, BOIS DE BRAY for duty.	
			No 3359 " HALL S.W. slightly wounded on head. Remained at duty.	
	8.7.16		No 2950 " GALE A.R. awarded 7 days C.B. for neglect of duty.	
FERME DOFFINE	10.7.16	2.30-3.30 p.m.	Town shelled. No material damage.	
MONT ST ELOY		5 pm	No 2704 L/Cpl MOODY H.W. reported to Lt. TURNER, 2/4th Lon 2nd Co R.E. for duty at Anketton Group.	
	11.7.16	11 am	No 984 Spr ROGERS A.D. reported to 25th Lond Ambce for duty at Pumping Station, HAUTE-AVESNES.	
		12 noon	Section officers met at Company Headquarters	
	12.7.16	8 am	Took over Stores & workshops f 2/2nd Highland Field E R.E. Took over work on Trent line & trenches.	
			No 2745 L/Cpl STREETER D.G. Admitted 2/5th London Field Ambce.	
	13.7.16	9 am	Took over Headquarters, Horse Lines & Intments from 2/2nd Highland Field Co. R.E.	
		4 pm	Transport, under 2/Lt E.H.J. STEWART, arrived from FERME DOFFINE.	

Army Form C. 2118

WAR DIARY
INTELLIGENCE SUMMARY
(Erase heading not required.)

Instructions regarding War Diaries and Intelligence Summaries are contained in F.S. Regs., Part II. and the Staff Manual respectively. Title Pages will be prepared in manuscript.

Place	Date	Hour	Summary of Events and Information	Remarks and references to Appendices
MONT ST ELOY.	14.7.16	9 a.m.	No 2722 Spr LUMB J.H. reported to O/C 8 Co Sig for duty (draughtsman)	
	16.7.16	6 p.m.	1 N.C.O. & 12 men from 2/18th Battn. L/Cpl THOMSON J.R. & 3 men from Regt. reported for working duties at R.E. Dump. BOIS DE BRAY.	
	17.7.16		No 2765 Cpl THOMSON J.R. & 3 men reported to O/C Light Railway, BOIS DE BRAY.	
	18.7.16	8 a.m.	No 2745 L/Cpl STREETER D.G. discharged hospital to duty. 1 N.C.O. & 17 men from 180th Inf. Bde reported for duty at R.E. Dump, BOIS DE BRAY.	
			No 2665 Spr STRINGER H.C. admitted hospital	
	19.7.16	8 a.m.	No 2697 Spr FLYNN W.T. awarded 7 days C.B. for insolence to a N.C.O. Working party 2/18th Battn. relieved by similar party of 2/19th Battn.	
		12 noon	L/Cpl MOODY H.W. returned to Unit from 2nd Londons Field Ct. H?	
	21.7.16	5 p.m.	No 2772 Cpl CLEMENT L.J. admitted hospital & evacuated to 42nd Cas. Clearing Station. Lieut. B.F. NELL, No 2204 2/Cpl ADAMS W.E. & 2704 L/Cpl MOODY H.W. proceeded to Div. Anti-gas School for course.	
	22.7.16		1 N.C.O. from 2/18th Battn attached for work at R.Q. Adv. Coy HQrs.	
	25.7.16	9 p.m.	2/Lt. E.H.J. STEWART proceeded from Rear Coy HQrs. to Front line for duty with section. Lieut. B.F. NELL & 2 N.C.O.s returned from Divnl Anti-gas School. Cpl THOMSON & 4 men returned from attachment to O/C Light Railway	
	26.7.16		No 2866 Spr HALL J.W. admitted hospital & evacuated to 30 Cas. Clearing Stn.	
	27.7.16		No 2765 Cpl THOMSON J.R. admitted hospital.	
	28.7.16	8 a.m.	Working party 2/19th Battn received by party of similar strength from 2/17th Battn. Lieut. B.F. NELL proceeded from Rear Coy HQrs. to Front line. 2/Lt W.H. LEE L/Cpl GREEN & L/Cpl LAURANTE returned to Rear Coy HQrs.	
	30.7.16	9 p.m.	Interpreter M COURRIER admitted to Hospital. 2/Lt W.H. LEE, L/Cpl GREEN & L/Cpl LAURANTE proceeded to Div Anti-gas School for course	

O.C. 1/6th London Field Coy. R.E.

1875 Wt. W593/826 1,000,000 4/15 J.B.C. & A. A.D.S.S./Forms/C. 2118.

Confidential

1/6th London Field Coy R.E.

War Diary

August 1916.

Army Form C. 2118

WAR DIARY
INTELLIGENCE SUMMARY
(Erase heading not required.)

Instructions regarding War Diaries and Intelligence Summaries are contained in F.S. Regs., Part II. and the Staff Manual respectively. Title Pages will be prepared in manuscript.

Place	Date	Hour	Summary of Events and Information	Weather	Remarks and references to Appendices
MONT ST ELOY	1/8/16		No 2771 Spr WATSON F.J. awarded 4 days C.B. by O.C. Coy for neglect of duty. "2700 Spr HICKS W Admitted Hospital (P.V.O) Loading Party, 1 NCO & 12 men from 2/7th Batt. Lon Regt, relieved by 2 NCOs & 21 men from Convalescent Co. Section No 1 proceeded to Rear Coy HQrs for Rest.	Fine	AW.D
	2/8/16		No 2766 Spr BURROWS W. admitted Hospital. 2nd Lieut W.H.LEE, No 2688 L/Cpl GREEN W.N.T Cloudy and No 2839 L/Cpl LAURANTE G. returned to Unit from Course at Staff Anti Gas School (Clear night)	Wind S-SE	AW.D
	3/8/16		No 2787 Spr LAUGHTON H.G. admitted hospital No 984 Spr ROGERS A.D returned to Unit from attached to 2/1st Ind Field Ambce for duty at Pumping Station. Section No 1 returned to Trenches	Fine	AW.D
	4/8/16		No 2700 Spr HICKS W. discharged hospital to duty. Section No 4 proceeded to Rear Coy HQrs for rest.	Fine Cloudy late	AW.D
	5/8/16	3.40pm	2/Lieut C.B TAYLOR (Second-in-Command) vacated Advance Coy HQrs. No 2941 Spr CLARKE C.F (Shell Shock) & No 3283 Spr MAYHEW W admitted hospital. "Gasalert" ordered from Right; + cancelled 3.45pm 2/Lieut W.H.LEE proceeds from Rear to Advanced Coy HQrs for duty. Reinforcement, No 3577 Spr HAMPSON. H. reported for duty. Capt D.H STEERS (O.C.Coy) promoted Temp Major as from 30/6/16.	Fine	AW.D
	6/8/16		No 891 Spr WARNE G.H.E & No 2660 Pnr SIMMONS C.E. admitted hospital. No 2766 Spr BURROWS W & Intrepete COURRIER discharged hospital to duty. Section No 4 returned to trenches	Fine	AW.D
	7/8/16		Section No 3 proceeded from Advances to Rear Coy HQrs for rest. Lieut B.F.NELL proceeded from Advances to Rear Coy HQrs to rest. No 2830 Spr GALE.G	Fine	AW.D
	8/8/16	10pm	See above from ECOIVRES (informed) + No 3266 Spr FOSTER D. admitted hospital	Fine Cloudy later	AW.D

WAR DIARY
INTELLIGENCE SUMMARY

(Erase heading not required.)

Army Form C. 2118

Instructions regarding War Diaries and Intelligence Summaries are contained in F.S. Regs., Part II. and the Staff Manual respectively. Title Pages will be prepared in manuscript.

Place	Date	Hour	Summary of Events and Information	Weather	Remarks and references to Appendices
MONS ST ELOY	9/8/16		No 2698 Sjt BLIZARD M.A. proceeded to R.E. School, an Instructor. Lieut W B BACON proceeded from Advance to Rear Coy HQrs for rest. Section No 3 returned to trenches.	Fine	N.9
	10/8/16		No 2772 Cpl CLEMENT L.J. discharged hospital to duty. Section No 2 proceeded to Rear Coy HQrs for rest.	do	N.9
	11/8/16		No 2765 Cpl THOMSON J.R. discharged hospital to duty. Reinforcements, N.S. Bts. Spr MITCHELL W.P. & No 3020 Spr FIELD R.E. reported for duty.	do	N.9
	12/8/16		No 2740 Spr HICKS W. admitted hospital. Section No 2 returned to trenches.	do	N.9
	13/8/16		No 2841 Spr ANDERSON J. commenced 14 days Course in Cookery at B" Army HQrs. 2/Lt A H LEE proceeded	low cloud some rain	N.9
	14/8/16		No 2660 Spr SIMMONS C.E. discharged hospital to duty. Section No 1 proceeded to Rear Coy HQrs for rest.	fine, some rain later	N.9
	15/8/16		No 2790 Spr HICKS W. discharged hospital to duty. Section No 1 proceeded to Rear Coy HQrs for rest. Lieut B.F.NELL, No 2246 Sjt CLARKE E.H. & 2661 Spr ROGERS F.W. commenced Commencing Crater Demolition at R.E. School.	showery and dull	N.9
	16/8/16		Section No 1 returned to trenches.	do	N.9
	17/8/16		2/Lt C.B.TAYLOR promoted temporary Captain to bear date 28/6/16. Section No 4 proceeded to Rear Coy HQrs for rest.	do	N.9
	18/8/16	9-10 am	About 15 shells from a S.9 gun fired onto MONT ST ELOY. No material damage. No 2700 Spr HICKS W & No 3002 Spr GRIMSLEY J. admitted hospital. Reinforcement, No 3044 Spr BATES A.E. reported for duty. Lieut R.F.NELL and Lieut W.B.BACON proceeded from Rear to Advance Coy HQrs for duty.	do	N.9

Army Form C. 2118

WAR DIARY
INTELLIGENCE SUMMARY
(Erase heading not required.)

Instructions regarding War Diaries and Intelligence Summaries are contained in F. S. Regs., Part II. and the Staff Manual respectively. Title Pages will be prepared in manuscript.

Place	Date	Hour	Summary of Events and Information	Weather	Remarks and references to Appendices
MONT ST ELOY	20/8/16		No 3283 Spr MAYHEW.W. discharges hospital to duty. 2/L E.H.J STEWART proceeded from advanced to Rear Coy HQrs for rest. Section No 4 returned to trenches.	Fine	OWD
	21/8/16		No 2830 Spr GALE.G. and No 3266 Spr FOSTER.D. discharges hospital to duty. 2/Lieut B.E. MORGAN reported for duty. 2/Lieut A.H LEE proceeded from Rear to advanced Coy HQrs for duty. Section No 3 proceeded to Rear HQrs for rest.	do	OWD
	22/8/16	8 pm	Hostile aircraft over BRAY, driven off by gunfire	do	OWD
	24/8/16		8 men from 180 Inf Bde attached for work & returns. Section No 3 returns to trenches	Cloudy wind WSW	OWD
	25/8/16	8 pm	2 Shrapnel Shells on BOIS DE BRAY. No damage. Capt C.B.TAYLOR worked advanced Cy HQrs	Fine showers later	OWD
	26/8/16	8 pm	One shell on BOIS DE BRAY. No damage. No 2700 Spr HICKS W discharges hospital to duty. 2/Lieut W.H. LEE and Section No 2 proceeded to Rear Coy HQrs for rest. Promotions made as per Appdix	Showery	OWD App. I
	27/8/16		2/Lieut E.H.J STEWART returned to trenches. No 2841 Spr ANDERSON J returns to duty from Cooking Course.	do	OWD
	28/8/16		2/Lieut B.E. MORGAN commenced Course at 2nd Army RE School. Lieut B.F. NELL attached to 1st RE HQrs temporary. — Salman No 2776 Spr JANNAWAY W. accompanying	Heavy showers	OWD
	29/8/16	10 am	Horse No 17785 (Bay Gelding) died. No 3359 Spr HALL S.W Discharged hospital to duty. No 2 Section returns to trenches.	do	OWD
	30/8/16		Section No 1 proceeded to Rear Coy HQrs for rest.	Heavy rain	OWD
	31/8/16	9 am	Hostile aircraft over MONT ST. ELOY Driven off by gunfire.	Fine	OWD

No 1 London Field Co R.E.
Appendices to War Diary
August 1916

Appendix I

Extract from 60th Divl. Engineer Routine Orders No 12 dated 26/8/16:–

The undermentioned NCO's are promoted to Acting Ranks as stated, & will be obeyed as such accordingly.

No 2744	Cpl DAWES H	Promoted Acty Sergeant	26/8/16
2743	2Cpl QUAINTANCE W.S.	do do Corpl	do
2656	2/cpl PEPPER W.E.	do do 2/cpl	do
2827	" HICKS T	do do do	do

The undermentioned men are appointed to Acting Rank as stated, & will be obeyed as such accordingly.

869	Spr BLUETT W.H.	Apptd Lce Cpl	26/8/16
2770	" QUAINTANCE A.E.	do do	do
2844	Dvr HAYDEN W	do do	do

Appendix 2.

Work during August 1916

Repairs to front line trenches carried on throughout the month.

Work on Forward Water Supply carried on from 5th to 31st August 1916.

Alterations to 180 Inf. Bde Advanced HQrs carried on from 9th to 31st August 1916.

Improvements to RE Dugouts effected 17th to 25th Aug '16.

Mortuary, ECOIVRES Cemetery, erected 6th to 17th Aug '16

Pump & piping installed at Baths. ACQ

31/8/16

RE 4

Confidential

War Diary

of

16th London Field Coy. R.E. (T.F.)

September, 1916.

WAR DIARY
INTELLIGENCE SUMMARY.
(Erase heading not required.)

Army Form C. 2118.

Instructions regarding War Diaries and Intelligence Summaries are contained in F.S. Regs., Part II. and the Staff Manual respectively. Title pages will be prepared in manuscript.

Place	Date	Hour	Summary of Events and Information	Weather	Remarks and references to Appendices
MONT ST ELOY	1/9/16	-	-	Fine	C.W.O
	2/9/16	9 p.m	Section No 1 returned to trenches	Fine	C.W.O
	3/9/16		No 2841 Spr ANDERSON J attached to Div HQrs RE HQrs	Fine	
			" 2772 Cpl CLEMENT L.J & No 2756 Spr BOULDEN T.A admitted Hospital		C.W.O
			2nd Lieut B.E MORGAN proceeded to A Co Hqrs for duty		
			Section No 4 proceeded to Rear Coy HQrs for rest.		
	4/9/16		2nd Lieut W.H. LEE returned to trenches	Rain	C.W.O
	5/9/16		No 3577 Spr HAMPSON H.G. proceeded on Special leave	Rain	
			Lieut W.B. BACON proceeded to Rear Coy HQrs for rest		C.W.O
			No 2772 Cpl CLEMENT L.J & No 2786 Spr BOULDEN T.A evacuated to 42nd Can Cy Stn		
			2 Horses (riders) taken over to complete establishment.		
	6/9/16		1 N.C.O 10 Drivers, 1 horse & 15 mules attached to 2/4 London Field Co RE	Fine	
			Lieut B.F NELL proceeded from Div RE HQrs to Staff Consolidation School		C.W.O
			No 2841 Spr ANDERSON J proceeded from Div RE HQrs to Third Army Rest Camp		
			for Special duty		
			Section No 4 returned to trenches		

Army Form C. 2118.

WAR DIARY
INTELLIGENCE SUMMARY.
(Erase heading not required.)

Instructions regarding War Diaries and Intelligence Summaries are contained in F.S. Regs., Part II. and the Staff Manual respectively. Title pages will be prepared in manuscript.

Place	Date	Hour	Summary of Events and Information	Weather	Remarks and references to Appendices
MONT ST ELOY	7/9/16	8pm	Major D.H. STEERS, O.C. Coy, proceeded from Advanced to Rear Coy H.Qrs	Fine	A1D
		7.30pm	Reinforcements, No. 2875 Spr BENNETT F. & No. 3000 Spr DOUBLE V.D.E. reported Section No 3 proceeded to Rear Coy H.Qrs for rest		
	8/9/16	2pm	Capt. C.B. TAYLOR, Second-in-Command, proceeded from Rear to Advanced Coy H.Qrs	Fine	A1D
			No 1226 Sgt HILBORNE S.C. attached to 3rd R.E. School for duty, returning		
			No 2698 Sgt BLIZARD H.A, returned to Unit		
	9/9/16		No 2700 Spr HICKS W commenced course at 3rd Army School of Cookery	Fine	A1D
			No 2826 Spr KEMP S.J. admitted hospital		
			Reinforcement No 3002 Spr GRIMSLEY J reported		
	10/9/16		No 2909 Spr DYKE A.W & No 2830 Spr GALE G. admitted hospital	Fine	A1D
			No 2826 Spr KEMP S.J evacuated to 30th Cas Clg Stn.		
			No 2798 Spr HICKS F. charged with neglecting to obey Standing orders awarded 14 days deprivation of Pay by O.C. Coy. Section No 3 returned to Trenches		
	11/9/16		Major D.H. STEERS, O.C. Coy, returned to Advanced Coy H.Qrs & Capt. C.B. TAYLOR to Rear Coy H.Qrs	Fine showers later	A1D
			2nd Lieut R.C. CASE & 32 other ranks of 3/3rd London Field Co R.E. and 2nd Lt A.F. NEAL, 2nd Lt C.G. JONES & 54 other ranks of 3/4 Lon Field Co R.E. attached for work on Gun Emplacements		

Army Form C. 2118.

WAR DIARY
or
INTELLIGENCE SUMMARY.
(Erase heading not required.)

Instructions regarding War Diaries and Intelligence Summaries are contained in F. S. Regs., Part II. and the Staff Manual respectively. Title pages will be prepared in manuscript.

Place	Date	Hour	Summary of Events and Information	[Weather]	Remarks and references to Appendices
MONT ST ELOY	12/9/16		9 BS[appers], 1 NCO + 18 Drivers + 37 Horses from 60th D.R.C. attached for transport of material for Gun Emplacement Works.	Dull	App.
			Lieut W.B. BACON returned to trenches. No 3877 Spr HAMPSON H.S. returned from Gas		
	13/9/16		No 2841 Spr ANDERSON J. returned from 3rd Army H.Qrs. to Dr/B H.Qrs	Dull	App
			No 2830 Spr GALE G. discharged hospital to duty.		
	14/9/16		No 2818 Spr KEEVILL L (under age) proceeded to 3rd Army Infantry School	Well	App
			No 2819 Spr RHODES D.W.H. admitted hospital		
			2nd Lieut A.H. OXLEY and 40 other ranks from 30th D.R.C. attached for work on Gun Emplacements		
	15/9/16		2nd Lieut E.H.T. STEWART with Natives, proceeded to Special Works Park, Hermaville	Fine	App
			to commence Course of Instruction		
	16/9/16		No 2819 Spr RHODES D.W.H. discharged hospital to duty	Fine	App
	17/9/16		2nd Lieut A.H. OXLEY and 40 other ranks returned to 30th D.A.C.	Fine	App
	18/9/16		2 NCOs + 13 men from M60 T.M Battery attached for work on Gun Emplacements	Very wet	App
			No 2710 Spr KIRKPATRICK G.L, No 3195 Spr ANDERSON S, + No 2977 Spr FARRER W. admitted hospital.		
	19/9/16		2/Lieut E.H.T. STEWART with Natives returned from Special Works Park.	Some showers	App
			Reinforcement No 3040 Spr HOYTE W. reported		

WAR DIARY

INTELLIGENCE SUMMARY

Army Form C. 2118.

Place	Date	Hour	Summary of Events and Information	Weather	Remarks and references to Appendices
MONT ST ELOY	20/9/16		4 Waggons, 8 horses & 2 G.S. waggons returned to 60th D.A.C. 2/Lieut E.H.I. STEWART proceeded to trenches for duty.	Showery	CWD
			No 2710 Gr KIRKPATRICK G.L. & No 2977 Dr FARRAR W evacuated to #2 Can Clg Stn	Dull	CWD
	21/9/16		1 NCO, 14 drivers, 29 horses & Y&S waggons returned to 60th Div A.C. 2/Lt A.F. NEAL, 246 C.G. JONES and 57 other ranks returned to 2/1st Lon Field CoRE		
			No 2689 Pnr BULLEN G admitted hospital. Gun Emplacements completed.		CWD
	22/9/16		2 NCOs - 13 men returned to W 60 T.M Battery	Fine	CWD
			No 2909 Dr DYKE A.W. discharged hospital to duty.		
	23/9/16		2/Lt R.C. CASE and 32 other ranks returned to 3/3rd London Field Co R.E. No 2700 Spr HICKS W returned from Third Army Cookery School	Fine	CWD
	25/9/16		No 2689 Pnr BULLEN G evacuated to 30th Can Clg Stn. No 3291 Spr A'BROOK F.H. attached to No 3 Coy A.S.C. for loading rations.	Fine	CWD
	26/9/16		No 3195 Pnr ANDERSON S. discharged hospital (Etaples) returned to Regt. returned to their Battalion 1 NCO & 2 men of 2/23rd Battalion for duty	Fine	CWD
			Reinforcements reported. No 2906 L/Cpl BEECHES T. 3451 Spr NORDEN S.A. & 2930 Spr BURGE E.B. No 3991 Rfn DILLON J & No 3104 Rfn BROWN E. 2/18 Batt Lon Regt (attached) charged with neglecting to obey Standing Orders, & marched Ydays C.B. by O.C. Coy		CWD

WAR DIARY
INTELLIGENCE SUMMARY
(Erase heading not required.)

Army Form C. 2118.

Place	Date	Hour	Summary of Events and Information	Remarks and references to Appendices
MONT ST ELOY	27/9/16		No. 2825 Spr NICHOLS E. admitted hospital	(ill)
	28/9/16		13 men of party attacked for breaking shutters at 6. 2/17th Batt. Lond. Shot from 1 of 2/14, 1 of 2/20, 1 of 2/13, 3 of 2/15, and 1 of 2nd Batt London Regt returned to their Battalions.	(iii)
			3 men of 2/17th Batt. & 1 man of 2/18th Batt London Regt attached for duty	
	30/9/16	10am	Camp fullets horse lines dug up for pickets established as proposed by G.O.C. 60th Division	(iv)
			Reinforcement No. 2977 Spr FARRAR W. reported from Convalescent Company	
			No. 2828 Spr NICHOLS E. discharged hospital to duty	

For O.C. 1/6th LONDON FIELD COY. R.E.T.
A.W. Taylor
CAPTAIN.

APPENDIX.

Work during the month.

Repairs to front support & communication trenches carried on throughout the month.

Construction of 13 Light T.M. Emplacements from 10/9/16 to 27/9/16
Construction of 2 Heavy T.M. Emplacements from 16/9/16 to 28/9/16
Construction of 10 Dugouts on front line from 3/9/16 to 30/9/16
Construction of 6 - 18 pdr Emplacements at F.3.6.9.8.3. end of
6 - 4.5 Howitzer Emplacements at F.2.a.7.6. from 12/9/16 to 21/9/16.
Work on forward water supply carried on throughout the month

Vol 5

Confidential

War Diary

of

1/6th London Field Co. R.E. (T.)

1st to 31st October 1916.

Army Form C. 2118.

WAR DIARY
or
INTELLIGENCE SUMMARY.
(Erase heading not required.)

Instructions regarding War Diaries and Intelligence Summaries are contained in F. S. Regs., Part II. and the Staff Manual respectively. Title pages will be prepared in manuscript.

Place	Date	Hour	Summary of Events and Information	Weather	Remarks and references to Appendices
MONT ST ELOY	1/10/16	9am	No 2723 Spr MUNDY A.P. proceeded to First Army H.Qrs. (workings)	fine	
			No 2875 Spr BENNETT F. & No 2851 Spr PATTERSON T.C. admitted Hospital		
	2/10/16		No 2825 Spr NICHOLS E. admitted hospital	wet	
		4pm	2nd Coy, reinforcements attached (which) from 180th Inf. Bde. 6 from 217th Batt? 6 from		
			218th Batt? 6 from 3/9th Batt? 3 & 6 from 3/20th Batt? under Regiment		
	3/10/16	12am	No 2154 Pnr BULLEN C. (reinforcement) reported	wet	
			No 2798 Spr HICKS F. admitted hospital		
	5/10/16	3pm	No 2844 Cpl BETON H.J. proceeded to 60th Div? F.E. School for study.	showery	
			Returning No 1226 Sgt HILBORNE S.C. returned to unit		
			2Lt W.H. LEE proceeded from Cateau went to Rear Coy.H.Qrs		
	6/10/16	3pm	2Lt W.H. LEE with others to leave to proceed to 60th Div? H.Q. 2nd Vol July	dull	
		6pm	Reinforcement No 2718 Spr KIRKPATRICK G.L. reported	windy	
			Lieut. B. BACON designated hospital		
	7/10/16	6pm	Lieut. B. BACON discharged hospital	wet	
			20 men of 2/4th Motor Ambulance Convoy attached for duty		
	8/10/16	11am	No 2851 Spr PATTERSON T.C. discharged hospital to duty	wet	

WAR DIARY
or
INTELLIGENCE SUMMARY.
(Erase heading not required.)

Army Form C. 2118.

Place	Date	Hour	Summary of Events and Information	Remarks and references to Appendices
MONT ST ELOY	9/10/18	4 pm	No 2046 Pte GREGORY J.W.R. Pte Roux attached ceased to be employed at	
		6 pm	Lieut B.F. NEAL went north between with Wheel party returned from attach to R.E. School	
	10/10/18	10 am	Lieut N.B. BACON proceeded home for 14 days army leave in UK	
	11/10/18	4 pm	Attached party from 2nd MAC relieved by army as forming	
	12/10/18		Corp. G.S. Wagstaff[?] returned to 60-DAC	
	13/10/18		No 2046 Pte GREGORY J.W.R. (Rome) ceased to be attached to be employed	
			A.O. 2819 Pte RHODES D.W.H. & A.O.2394 Pte KEANEY A.A. admitted to ? ill	
	14/10/18	10 am	Reinforcements Lieut SO ANDERSON & A.L. 327 - Pte BANNETT F.	
	15/10/18	4 pm	Attached party from 2nd MAC relieved by reinforcements	
	16/10/18		Equipment of Company checked & deficiencies noted	
	17/10/18		Lieut SD ANDERSON commenced course at [?] R.E. School	
			Reinforcements A.L. 325 Pte NICHOLS E. A.L. 2455 Pte SWADLING R. ? duty 260	
			Capt. HARMER F.E. reported.	
	18/10/18	4 pm	Attached party from 2nd MAC relieved by reinforcements on ? for	
	2/10/18		No 2819 Pte RHODES D.W.H. discharged to duty (they ? tried	
		10.30pm	2nd Lieut V.A. LEE arrived between here in the bridge? Returned in ? ? ?	

WAR DIARY
INTELLIGENCE SUMMARY.
(Erase heading not required.)

Army Form C. 2118.

Place	Date	Hour	Summary of Events and Information	Remarks and references to Appendices
MONT ST ELOY	20/10/16	11am	Attached Infantry working parties returned to Battalions — 15 men to 2/17 Batt. — 18 men to 2/18th Batt. — 13 men to 2/19 Batt. — 12 men to 2/20 & 14th Lon. Regt.	
		6.30pm	No. 2722 Sgt LUMB J.M. returned from attachment to Div. Pok H.Qrs. No. 27 L/Cpl SNEE A. and J. Shoesmith L. Corp. 13 weeks Rd. Course from attachment to 2/4 London Field Co. R.E. Course No. 3177 O Sgt MARSH E. and two sick men to R.H.F.S.K. & 7 P.B.B. Two L/S horses No. 2 17750 - 177-5 L.S. to Middle Veterinary Hosp. 60th Sir Engineer order No. 2 received — 60th Div. (Obs Aucklen) to be relieved by 3rd Canadian Division (Inv Artillery) during 23/26 Field 1916 the relief being by 3rd Canadian Division. No. 1163 Cadet S field Con R.B. to be relieved by 7th Can. Lancers 1C.G. O.C. 4th Canadian Field Co. arrived here 2 hour & reported and 6.30.	
	22/10/16	2pm	Reinforcement No 2798 Spr MUSSEL F. reported.	
		3pm	Remounting attached temporarily working party relieved Co B & Lancer. 6 men to 3/17 Batt Infantry. 4 2/18 Batt. 13 men to 14 Lon. Regt. 12 to 2/19 — to 2/4th Lond Field Co RE	
	23/10/16	9am	Kent B. O'NEIL. transferred to 2/4 London Field Co. R.E. two L.S. No. 1 176 and No. 17849 sent here to Cale. A 1/3am sick to H666 & Cavalry Section	

Army Form C. 2118.

WAR DIARY
INTELLIGENCE SUMMARY.
(Erase heading not required.)

Instructions regarding War Diaries and Intelligence Summaries are contained in F. S. Regs., Part II. and the Staff Manual respectively. Title pages will be prepared in manuscript.

Place	Date	Hour	Summary of Events and Information	Remarks and references to Appendices
MONT ST ELOY	23/4/16			
PENIN				
VOLCHELLES	27/4/16			
MONCHEAUX				
RANTIERES				
FAMECHON				

Army Form C. 2118.

WAR DIARY
or
INTELLIGENCE SUMMARY.
(Erase heading not required.)

Instructions regarding War Diaries and Intelligence Summaries are contained in F.S. Regs., Part II. and the Staff Manual respectively. Title pages will be prepared in manuscript.

Place	Date	Hour	Summary of Events and Information	Remarks and references to Appendices
FAVECHON	2/4/16	6.45am	Lieut. S.D. ANDERSON & 2Lieut. W.M. LEE took Section No 3, Motor Transport	Weather
			& 2 Lorries proceeded to BERTRANCOURT for duty under O.C. VII Corps Headquarters.	Some showers
		3pm	2Lieut. E.H.T. STEWART with Section No 4, Motor Transport proceeded to MARIEUX for period of attachment to 11th Army Troops Company.	

O.C. 170th LONDON FIELD COY. R.E.T.

MAJOR

T2134. Wt. W708—776. 500000. 4/15. Sir J. C. & S.

Army Form C. 2118.

WAR DIARY
or
INTELLIGENCE SUMMARY.
(Erase heading not required.)

Place	Date	Hour	Summary of Events and Information	Remarks and references to Appendices
			Aberdeen	
			Appendix 1. Mon 23/10/16 MONT ST ELOY to PENIN	
			Route - MONT ST ELOY - ACQ - [illegible] ARRAS-STRN and AGR HAUTE AVESNES Roads in SAVY -	App.
			BERLES - PENIN	
			Appendix 2. Mon 26/10/16 PENIN to MONCHEAUX	
			Route - PENIN - MAIZIERES - GOUY-EN-TERNOIS - MONTS-EN-TERNOIS - MONCHEAUX	App.
			Appendix 3. Mon 28/10/16 MONCHEAUX to BONNIERES	
			Route: MONCHEAUX - HOUVIN-HOUVIGNEUL - REBREUVIETTE - GRAND-PUSET - ESTREE - BONNIERES	App.
			Appendix 4. Mon 29/10/16 BONNIERES to FAMECHON	
			Route - BONNIERES - [illegible] - FREVENT - DOULLENS and BONNIERES - REBREUVIETTE Roads	App.
			West of M. on M. LEBLOND - HASTE VINES - GROUCHES - L'ESPERANCE - HALLY - FAMECHON.	

[signature] Major
O.C. 178th [illegible] 1st Div. R.E.T.

WAR DIARY
or
INTELLIGENCE SUMMARY.
(Erase heading not required.)

Army Form C. 2118.

Place	Date	Hour	Summary of Events and Information	Remarks and references to Appendices

Appendix 5

Work during the month

Work on construction of dugouts in front line carried on from 1st to 21st Oct from 1st to 21st Oct

Work on BIRMINGHAM Water Scheme carried on from 1st to 21st Oct

Revetting trench ROSS St.   do

Repairing Boilers & drying rooms at Baths NEUVILLE from 1st to 17th Oct

Excavating Power House dugout AUX RIETZ from 1st to 12th Oct

Repairing WINCHESTER HOUSE from 3rd to 12th Oct

Repairing trench RENT St. from 8th to 21st Oct

Cutting for Railway CROSS Sd. from 1st to 3rd Oct

Repairing Checko Dugouts R.E. Horse from 5th to 17th Oct

Work on RAMC Railway QUARRIES from 9th to 31st Oct

Work on NEUVILLE Railway 18th to 20th Oct

Construction of shelters 3rd TM Emplacements from 13th to 21st Oct

Appendix 3

NOMINAL ROLL of DRIVERS TRANSFERRED FROM 1/8th LONDON FIELD COY. R.E. to HEADQUARTERS, 60th Divsl. Engnrs. with teams for PONTOON, TRESTLE, LIMBERED R.E. and SEARCHLIGHT WAGONS. Vide War Establishment, Part 1?.

2759.	Dvr.	Smith W.D.
3186.	"	Wilson A.J.
2774.	"	Long S.G.
3178.	"	Mattey B.
2819.	"	Rhodes D.W.R.
3157.	"	Fowler H.
2771.	"	Watson F.J.
3039.	"	Dawe H.A.
2733.	"	McCormack W.J.
2123.	"	Spencer E.H.
2685.	"	Hughes J.H.
2842.	"	Parslow A.
2685.	"	Young D.J.E.
2775.	"	Wadlow T.H.
2707.	"	Davies J.T.
2909	"	Dyke A.W.

Vol 6

Confidential

War Diary

of

1/1st London Field Coy. R.E.

1st to 30th November 1916

WAR DIARY
—or—
INTELLIGENCE SUMMARY.
(Erase heading not required.)

Army Form C. 2118.

Place	Date	Hour	Summary of Events and Information	Remarks and references to Appendices
FAMECHON	1/11/16		No. 2773 Pte SANDERS C.T. admitted to C.C.S. sick bronchitis	
		3 p.m.	Lieut J.O. ANDERSON, 2nd Lieut W. HEE & Section No 3 returned from BERTANGLES	
	2/11/16	3 a.m.	2nd Lieut E.H.T. STEWART & Section No.4 returned from MOLLIENS	
		"	Company moved to MAILLARD-bivouacked (entrained at Longeau)	
			Route:- (Mes LENS 1) FAMECHON-THIEVRES-ORVILLE-DOULLENS-GÉZAI -OUTREBOIS-LE MEILLARD entrained LE MEILLARD 3.20 pm	
			Rank By. Major No. 17781 injured on road & left with No. 29 G.B. HARVEY AV. charged with valuables	
			The march through somewhere & Army Ser Corps through LeMeillard Lane	
		3:30pm	Awarded 7 days for absence of kit by OC Company Reinforcements 3 NCOs 40 men T OTTERSON 373 1463 Pte DAVIS E.T. Trans from	
LE MEILLARD	3/11/16	9am	Company marched to BUSSUS-BUSSUEL, arrived 1pm. Route:- (Mes ABNS 11) LE MEILLARD - ?? - St VALERY - HEUZECOURT - Cross Roads S.E. of DROUVILLE - DROUVILLE - BOUVILLE - LONGVILLERS - DOMQUEUR - BUSSUS-BUSSUEL	
B. SUS. BUSSUE	4/11/16	10 am	Kit inspection No 2830 Pte GALE G admitted C.C.S. (in addition to Somebody)	

WAR DIARY or INTELLIGENCE SUMMARY

Army Form C. 2118.

Place	Date	Hour	Summary of Events and Information	Remarks and references to Appendices
BUSSUS BUSSUEL	4/1/16	8 pm	No 391 Pte COX W. and No 3354 Spr HALL S.W. returned from hospital	
	5/1/16		No 248 Spr BLIZARD H.A. and No 2746 Pte CARTER A.H. admitted to hospital	Showery
		2.45 pm	Checking & packing Company equipment	
	6/1/16		Cpls C.B. TAYLOR, Lieut W.B. BACON and 3 other ranks proceed to England on leave	
			30 Bracer Aiguilettes to DADOS 4th Army	
			1 Kirchoff EC bayonet with 2 scabbers and scraper sent to WS Coy RSC	
			(Casson) No 3841 Spr ANDERSON J. admitted to hospital & No 6 DF Coy	
			Sent B.S.VEST Thermos [illegible] to 1st [illegible] field for P.B. tender [illegible]	
			CRO Ctee A/13900/253 of 2/9/16, Strange [illegible] date 24/9/16 (... ...)	
			No 3076 Spr UNGLES H.R.H. transferred to Ordnance 2nd NCO and issued	
			for leave of 28 days pay [illegible] leave pay	
			4 Qr gauges 2 suitings KA [illegible] 2 [illegible] and 3 pol coats and a [illegible] list	
	8/1/16		Advanced on indent to Scott ADDITIONS	
			No 2651 2nd Cpl DEMPER W.B. and A.A. hospital As 1821 [illegible]	
			proceed to hospital. No 2846 1 Cpl MYERS H.A. No 215 Spr [illegible] Wt [illegible]	
			promoted Acting Cpl. No 2917 S/Smith HAMMOND H.C. promoted to [illegible]

WAR DIARY
or
INTELLIGENCE SUMMARY.
(Erase heading not required.)

Army Form C. 2118.

Place	Date	Hour	Summary of Events and Information	Remarks and references to Appendices
BUSSU BUSSUE	10/4/16	10am	Authorized G. COURIER to proceed via KOMA to PALA	
		10.30am	2 officers and 50 men were in advance and T.P. 3	
			20 L.D. were ordered off	
		10/4/16 7am	17 mules, unsuitable, dropped on the way	
			No. 2950 Pte GALE AR, admitted hospital	
			Landed in L. CAO.DS. list of same	
	11/4/16	10am	All horses mules unloaded. [illegible] and [illegible] [illegible]	
		10.30am	In GRIMSLEY T. arrived [illegible]. No.2776 Cr [illegible]	
			[illegible] splinter 20M Co 68. No.187 Pt GROVE F. AB. 9M	
			Engrs returned this evening and reported [illegible] Return	
		3pm	No. 3273 & TUREY A.P. admitted hospital	
		6.30pm	Reinforcements to [illegible] Col. No.166 L PEEL A. No.35.10 Pt SOUT [illegible] and a	
	12/4/16		Ord CB TAYLOR arrived. U.B. PASSY AR. [illegible]	
	13/4/16		2 Pon Cos & [illegible] & lieu came in with 30 [illegible]	
			and horses and 15 Askari being relieved &	
			Send one Battalion & one Oasr (2) to ack 4 [illegible] via [illegible]	

WAR DIARY
or
INTELLIGENCE SUMMARY.
(Erase heading not required.)

Army Form C. 2118.

Place	Date	Hour	Summary of Events and Information	Remarks and references to Appendices
BUSSUS BUSSUEL	13/4/16		Riding horse inspection carried out. Horses Detailed to Mobile Veterinary Section	
			No 300250 Pte FISHER E admitted to hospital	
	14/4/16	10 am	1 Riding horse transferred from 3/3 London Field Amb	
		2.30pm	No 25322 Farrier S/Sgt SIMPSON J.B. No 27452 Shoeing Smith D.G. and No 29775 Farrier W [illegible] admitted to hospital	
			Found unfit by Board at the time of Medical Board [illegible]	
			Proceeded to No 1 Southwark and to B.E. Authority A/DMS 60 Div M/1286 of 12/4/16	
		4 pm	3 Officers & 17 Other Ranks inoculated T.A.B.	
			3 Officers returned from leave	
			46 Drivers, 42 Mules & Pattern Wagons, 3 G.S. Wagons & limbers [illegible] Wagons from H.Q. Co 2nd Eng (Divn) at Isobel	
	15/4/16		2/Lieut W H LEES & batman proceeded to VARSEILLES en route to S.S. Rhoda [illegible] Embarkation Isobel	
			No 2895 Sgt MOSS T.W.F. & No 3003 Pte MOSEY A admitted to hosp.	
			1 Water Cart complete and 1 Forward Wagon to S/4 ASC E Coy A.S.C.	
	16/4/16		2 Mules with harness (complete with traces) and 1 S/4 HT Coy ASC	
			No 2656 2nd Cpl PEPPER W.E. admitted to hospital	

WAR DIARY
or
INTELLIGENCE SUMMARY.
(Erase heading not required.)

Army Form C. 2118.

Place	Date	Hour	Summary of Events and Information	Remarks and references to Appendices
BXXPS BOJOE	17/4/16		No 11101 Pte LAYTON #A (H&RE) No 8666 Pte CHERRIE HT & No 3353 Pte MARTIN W. admitted hospital. No 2450 Spr CAME AR discharged to duty.	
	18/4/16		No 12172 CQMS WHAMOND G.R. & 24 Horses Rfts O.R. & R.E. attached	
		3.45am	3 Officers 127 other Ranks & 10 horses, and 15 vehicles 92 mules struck attached from HQ 60 Ber RE. marched to Entraining Station LOVERS arriving from	
		7.15am	2 Officers, 99 otherranks + 110 animals marched to LONGPRE arriving 10.30am	
			ROUTE:- (Map ABBEVILLE) BUSSOS EUSSOE - YACOURT - AILLY EAST - YAUCHER - LONGPRE (17)	
		8.30pm	3 Officers, 136 other Ranks & 116 (excl R.E. and 1 Officer 60 other Ranks At 20	
			96 mules w 10 vehicles & 40 60 Ber Rens and 1 Mule (No 68) left from entraining	
		12mdt	2 Officers, 99 other Ranks & 20 horses w 10 mules entrained	
			5 limbers & go no left to proceed overland 1 NCO 7 men	
	19/4/16		army journey by travel 1 Mule (No 68) left from Entraining to Entraining	
	20/4/16		train journey continued.	
	21/4/16		2nd trainload arrived MARSEILLES	
		12noon	1st trainload arrived MARSEILLES	
		10.30am	4 officers, 181 other Ranks & 1 OR of 24 Agst Det. marched to MISSOT Camp	

WAR DIARY or INTELLIGENCE SUMMARY

Army Form C. 2118.

Place	Date	Hour	Summary of Events and Information	Weather	Remarks and references to Appendices
MARSEILLES	24/11/16		1 Officer, 37 other Ranks, 2nd Arrivals of 416 & and 48 sick, 1 officer 60 other Ranks 102 animals & 10 vehicles of 11KB (B proceeded to VALENTIN Camp	Fine	
	25/11/16	12.30pm	No 2754 Spr WALKER W.A. admitted hospital NCO & 6 men with 5 limbered GS wagons (MK.6) arrived		
			No 2701 A/Cpl MOODY H.W. admitted hospital		
	27/11/16		No 3047 Spr HYAMS A.F.G admitted to hospital	Fine	
			No 1108 Army Sergt Sergt ROSSIN A, A.O.C att whilst unable to join 2/L # B.th Lin Regt		
	28/11/16		No 2187 Spr LAUGHTON H.G. admitted hospital	do	
			Capt. C.B TAYLOR and 4 other Ranks embarked with H.Q (B 4th Echelon		
			1 NCO & 12 men proceeded from VALENTIN Camp to MUSSOT Camp.		
			Lieut S.D. ANDERSON with following proceeded from MUSSOT Camp to take charge of Mounted Detachment at VALENTIN Camp		
	29/11/16		No 3278 Spr GUY F.E. admitted hospital	do	
	30/11/16		No 2934 Spr WALSH M and No 3599 Spr BROWN T.W. admitted hospital	do	
	1/12/16		No 1629 Spr NOAKES A.F. admitted hospital	do	

Army Form C. 2118.

WAR DIARY
—or—
INTELLIGENCE SUMMARY.
(Erase heading not required.)

Instructions regarding War Diaries and Intelligence Summaries are contained in F. S. Regs., Part II. and the Staff Manual respectively. Title pages will be prepared in manuscript.

Place	Date	Hour	Summary of Events and Information	Remarks and references to Appendices
MARSEILLES	28/11/6		No 2660 Pte SIMMONS C.E admitted hospital	Weather
	29/11/6		" 2759 " WALKER W.A discharged hospital to duty	Fine
	30/11/6		" 2699 " CARTER W.H admitted hospital	Fine
			From 22nd Nov to 30th Nov Sections & Company H.Q's were established. Also pitching tents, electric lighting of Camp &c	Fine
	Note		The following Officers on attm to Battalion with 2nd Establishment Part (a) reported to 60 Details 179th Infantry Brigade unit leaving BUSCUS BUSSUS on 18th Nov for unknown 2nd Lieut F.H.J STEWART " B.E. MORGAN " W.I. STINSON	

J A Pleu
Major
O.C. 1/8th LONDON REG. R.F.A.